cool drinks

OVER 80 THIRST-QUENCHING
RECIPES TO KEEP YOU CHILLED

LINDA DOESER &
CHRISTINE AMBRIDGE

NOTE

*This book uses metric and imperial measurements. Follow the same units of
measurement throughout; do not mix metric and imperial. All spoon measurements
are level: teaspoons are assumed to be 5 ml and tablespoons are assumed to be 15 ml.
Unless otherwise stated, milk is assumed to be whole, eggs and individual vegetables
such as potatoes are medium, and pepper is freshly ground black pepper.*

*Recipes using raw or very lightly cooked eggs should be avoided by infants, the elderly,
pregnant women, convalescents, and anyone suffering from an illness. Pregnant and
breastfeeding women are advised to avoid eating peanuts and peanut products.*

Contents

Introduction

Nowadays supermarkets are crammed with bottles, cartons, and cans containing hundreds of different drinks, from fruit juices to flavored yogurts—even ready mixed cocktails.

Yet, somehow, they never quite live up to their labels and our expectations—they're too sweet, they lack "bite," or they taste like liquid bubble gum. There's a simple answer—get creative in the

kitchen—and you're holding the key in your hands with this book. Whether you want an energizing booster to start the day, a refreshing cooler in the midafternoon, a sophisticated cocktail to set the tone for the evening, or a nightcap to help you wind down, you will find the perfect recipe in the following pages.

This book is divided into two main sections. The first part is packed with recipes for classic and contemporary cocktails and even includes a chapter of "mocktails"—nonalcoholic mixed

drinks. Don't worry if you don't know your Piña Colada from your White Lady: there is helpful advice on what is stirred and what is shaken and how to do it.

The second section provides a cornucopia of recipes for smoothies and juices based on fresh fruit, vegetables, herbs, and spices, and coffee and chocolate to set the taste buds singing. A guide to techniques and equipment, much of which you will already have in your kitchen, guarantees success, whether you crave a healthy juice or a self-indulgent shake.

Cool in every sense, these drinks are just asking to be shared with friends and family. Cocktails are back in style and today's cocktail party has a new approach that matches the informality of modern life. You can, of course, still dress decadently and sip delicately at a Martini, but equally, you can push the boat out with a Full Monty and wear... whatever you like.

usually end up with boring bottled fruit juice and unexciting mineral water. Both the chapter of nonalcoholic cocktails and most of the second section of this book provide the answer to this dilemma—drinks with a sophisticated edge and adult appeal. Drivers may have to resist the temptation of a Singapore Sling or Bloody Mary, but they will be grateful if you offer them glasses of Grapefruit Cooler or Red Pepper Reactor.

Coolers and iced teas are the perfect choices for summer brunches and picnics, while a night in experimenting with a selection of smoothies is not just fun, but will make you feel virtuously healthy. You could even serve one of the savory vegetable smoothies as an unusual appetizer to an alfresco meal or end a summer supper with a refreshing glass of iced coffee.

While cocktails are colorful, festive, and delicious, not everyone wants alcoholic drinks, even at a party. It's often difficult to find nonalcoholic drinks to suit adults, and they

There are great recipes for the kids, too, from irresistible milkshakes to old-fashioned favorites such as Traditional Lemonade. Freshly made, with no artificial flavorings or colorings, and, in many instances, much more economical than commercial soft drinks, they're also packed full of vitamins. What parent could ask for more? Of course, kids just love the flavors and the fun.

None of these drinks are difficult to make and most are virtually instant—all you need is a good stock of ingredients. So whenever you are feeling thirsty, get shaking and stirring, juicing and whizzing for the perfect cool drink.

Cocktails

Precisely where the word "cocktail" came from is uncertain. A popular story describes how a Mexican princess called Xoctl offered a mixed drink to an American visitor to her father's court, who confused her name with that of the drink itself. Other suggestions are based on the fact that nonthoroughbred horses in the 18th- and 19th-centuries were referred to as being "cock-

tailed," because their tails looked like those of cockerels. Some say that these horses' docked tails also resembled the spoon used for mixing drinks, leading to imbibing racegoers using the term for the drinks as well; others say that the term for these mixed-blood horses seemed appropriate for drink made up of many different

substances. There are many other flights of fancy, but modern etymologists mostly agree that the word derives from *coquetel*, a French, wine-based drink.

Whatever the origins of the word cocktail, mixed drinks have existed since ancient times and the first recognizable cocktail dates from about the 16th century. Indeed, many

classics have been around for much longer than most people think. The bourbon-based Old Fashioned, for example, first appeared at the end of the 18th century. We know that the word cocktail was already in use in 1809 in the United States and, thirty-five years later, when Charles Dickens described Major Pawkins as able to drink "more rum-toddy, mint-julep, gin-sling, and cock-tail, than any private gentleman of his acquaintance," it had reached the other side of the Atlantic, too.

Popular among the style-conscious and wealthy in the United States, cocktails were served before dinner in the most exclusive houses and hotels until World War I made them unfashionable. They have gone in and out of vogue ever since.

Following the war, young people, disillusioned by the older generation and

desperately seeking new experiences, pleasures, stimuli, and styles, developed a taste for a new range of cocktails. Ironically, Prohibition in the United States in the 1920s spurred on their development. Illegally produced liquor frequently tasted poisonous—and sometimes was—so the clubs and speakeasies needed to disguise its flavor with fruit juices and mixers. No doubt, the naughtiness of drinking alcoholic cocktails also added to their appeal to the "bright young things" of the time. The craze quickly crossed the

Atlantic and the best hotels in London, Paris, and Monte Carlo, where the quality of gin and whiskey was more consistent, soon boasted their own cocktail bars.

World War II brought an end to such revelry and, although drunk occasionally, cocktails remained out of style for decades until an exuberant renaissance in the 1980s. This resulted in another new generation of recipes, often featuring white rum and vodka, as well as tequila, which was just becoming known outside its native Mexico. Inevitably, the pendulum swung again and cocktails fell from favor until recently. Now, once more, the cocktail shaker is essential equipment in every fashionable city bar.

Equipment

Classic cocktails are either shaken or stirred. A shaker is essential. It consists of a container with an inner, perforated lid and an outer lid. Both lids are secured while the mixture is shaken, together with cracked ice, and then the cocktail is strained through the perforated lid into a glass.

A mixing glass is a medium-size pitcher for preparing stirred cocktails. Uncolored glass is best, so you can see what you are doing.

A long-handled bar spoon is perfect for stirring and a small strainer prevents the ice cubes—used during mixing—finding their way into the cocktail glass. Some modern cocktails, and any cocktail that is made by shaking, can be made in a blender or food processor, so if you have one, by all means make use of it.

Measuring cups and spoons are essential for getting the proportions right—guessing does not work. A corkscrew, bottle-opener, and sharp knife are crucial.

You can serve cocktails in any glasses you like. Small, V-shaped, stemmed glasses may be worth buying, but it is not essential to have a full range of all the different glasses. Tumblers, small tumblers, and wine glasses cover most contingencies. As part of their appeal is visual, cocktails are best served in clear, uncut glass. Chill the glasses to ensure cocktails are cold.

Ingredients

You can stock your bar over a period of time with the basics—it is not necessary to buy everything at once. A good, all-round selection of alcoholic drinks would include whiskey, possibly Scotch and bourbon, brandy, gin, light and dark rum, triple sec, sweet and dry vermouth, vodka, and tequila. You could also include Pernod, beer, and wine. Keep champagne cocktails for special occasions.

Standard mixers include soda water, sparkling mineral water, cola, ginger ale, and tonic water. Freshly squeezed fruit juice is best, but when buying juice in a bottle or carton, avoid any with added sugar or extra "padding." Cranberry juice, for example, may be bulked with grape juice. Commercial brands of grapefruit, orange, cranberry, tomato juice, and lime cordial are also useful.

A good supply of fresh lemons, limes, and oranges is essential. Fresh fruit is best, but if you use canned, buy it in natural juice (not syrup) and drain well. Other garnishes and condiments include Angostura bitters, Worcestershire sauce, and maraschino cherries. Finally, you can never have too much ice.

Techniques

Store ice in the freezer before using. To crack ice, put ice cubes into a strong plastic bag and hit it against an outside wall, or put the ice between clean cloths on a sturdy surface and crush with a wooden mallet. Cracked ice is used in both shaken and stirred cocktails. To crush ice, crack it as before but break it into much smaller pieces. Use crushed ice in cocktails prepared in a blender.

Glasses can be frosted with sugars—or salt for Margaritas or Salty Dog. Rub the rim with a wedge of lemon or lime, then dip into a saucer of salt or superfine sugar until evenly coated.

To make sugar syrup, put 4 tablespoons each of water and superfine sugar into a pan. Stir over low heat until the sugar has dissolved. Bring to a boil, then boil, without stirring, for 1–2 minutes. Cool, then refrigerate in a covered container for up to 2 weeks .

To make a shaken cocktail, put cracked ice into a shaker and pour over the other ingredients. Secure the lids and shake vigorously for 20 seconds, or until a frost forms on the outside of the shaker. Strain into a glass and serve at once. To make a stirred cocktail, use fresh cracked ice and pour over the ingredients immediately. Using a long-handled spoon, stir vigorously, without splashing, for 20 seconds. Strain into a glass and serve at once.

Classic
Cocktails

Classic Cocktail

This cannot lay claim to being the first or even the only classic, but it has all the characteristic hallmarks of sophistication associated with cocktails.

serves 1

lemon wedge

1 tsp superfine sugar

4–6 cracked ice cubes

2 measures brandy

1/2 measure clear Curaçao

1/2 measure Maraschino

1/2 measure lemon juice

halved lemon slice, to decorate

❶ Rub the rim of a chilled cocktail glass with the lemon wedge, then dip in the sugar to frost.

❷ Put the cracked ice cubes into a cocktail shaker. Pour the brandy, Curaçao, Maraschino, and lemon juice over the ice and shake vigorously until a frost forms on the shaker.

❸ Strain into the frosted glass and decorate with the halved lemon slice.

Variations

A number of cocktails are the quintessential classics of their type and named simply after the main ingredient.

Champagne Cocktail: place a sugar cube in the bottom of a chilled champagne flute and dash with Angostura bitters to douse it. Fill the glass with chilled champagne and decorate with a lemon peel twist.

Tequila Cocktail: put 4–6 cracked ice cubes into a cocktail shaker. Dash Angostura bitters over the ice and pour in 3 measures golden tequila, 1 measure lime juice, and 1/2 measure grenadine. Shake vigorously until a frost forms, then strain into a chilled cocktail glass.

Brandy Cocktail: put 4–6 cracked ice cubes into a cocktail shaker. Dash Angostura bitters over the ice and pour in 2 measures brandy and 1/2 teaspoon sugar syrup (see page 11). Shake vigorously until a frost forms, then strain into a chilled cocktail glass and decorate with a twist of lemon.

Bartender's Tip

Maraschino is a sweet Italian liqueur made from cherries. It is usually white, but may also be colored red. The white version is better for most cocktails, because it does not affect the appearance of the finished drink.

Sidecar

Cointreau is the best-known brand of the orange-flavored liqueur known generically as triple sec. It is drier and stronger than Curaçao and is always colorless.

serves 1

4–6 cracked ice cubes
2 measures brandy
1 measure triple sec
1 measure lemon juice
orange peel twist, to decorate

❶ Put the cracked ice cubes into a cocktail shaker. Pour the brandy, triple sec, and lemon juice over the ice and shake vigorously until a frost forms.
❷ Strain into a chilled glass and decorate with the orange peel twist.

Variations

Champagne Sidecar: make a Sidecar as above, but strain it into a chilled champagne flute, and then top off with chilled champagne.

Chelsea Sidecar: put 4–6 cracked ice cubes into a cocktail shaker. Pour 2 measures gin, 1 measure triple sec, and 1 measure lemon juice over the ice. Shake vigorously until a frost forms, then strain into a chilled glass. Decorate with a lemon peel twist.

Boston Sidecar: put 4–6 cracked ice cubes into a cocktail shaker. Pour 1½ measures white rum, ½ measure brandy, ½ measure triple sec, and ½ measure lemon juice over the ice and shake vigorously until a frost forms. Strain into a chilled glass and decorate with an orange peel twist.

Polish Sidecar: put 4–6 cracked ice cubes into a cocktail shaker. Pour 2 measures gin, 1 measure blackberry brandy, and 1 measure lemon juice over the ice. Shake until a frost forms, then strain into a chilled glass. Decorate with a fresh blackberry.

Did you know?

You can buy "ice cubes" made from soapstone. Place them in the freezer to chill and use as you would ice cubes. They will not dilute your cocktails and will last forever.

Stinger

Aptly named, this is a refreshing, clean-tasting cocktail to tantalize the taste buds and make you sit up and take notice. However, bear in mind that it packs a punch; if you have too many, you are likely to keel over.

serves 1

4–6 cracked ice cubes
2 measures brandy
1 measure white crème de menthe

❶ Put the cracked ice cubes into a cocktail shaker. Pour the brandy and crème de menthe over the ice. Shake vigorously until a frost forms.
❷ Strain into a small, chilled glass.

Variations

Amaretto Stinger: put 4–6 cracked ice cubes into a cocktail shaker. Pour 2 measures Amaretto and 1 measure white crème de menthe over the ice. Shake vigorously until a frost forms, then strain into a chilled cocktail glass.

Chocolate Stinger: put 4–6 cracked ice cubes into a cocktail shaker. Pour 1 measure dark crème de cacao and 1 measure white crème de menthe over the ice. Shake vigorously until a frost forms, then strain into a chilled cocktail glass.

Irish Stinger: put 4–6 cracked ice cubes into a cocktail shaker. Pour 1 measure Bailey's Irish Cream and 1 measure white crème de menthe over the ice. Shake vigorously until a frost forms, then strain into a chilled shot glass.

Did you know?

Bailey's Irish Cream is the world's top-selling liqueur and accounts for 1 percent of the Irish Republic's export revenue.

American Rose

"A rose by any other name..."—this Oscar-winning cocktail has, rightly, inspired roses across the world. It is truly a thing of beauty and a joy forever.

serves 1

4-6 cracked ice cubes
1½ measures brandy
1 tsp grenadine
½ tsp Pernod
½ fresh peach, peeled and mashed
sparkling wine, to top off
fresh peach wedge, to decorate

❶ Put the cracked ice cubes into a cocktail shaker. Pour the brandy, grenadine, and Pernod over the ice and add the peach pulp. Shake vigorously until a frost forms.

❷ Strain into a chilled wine goblet and top off with sparkling wine. Stir gently, then decorate with the peach wedge.

Variations

White Rose: put 4–6 cracked ice cubes into a cocktail shaker. Dash lemon juice over the ice and pour in 3 measures gin, 1 measure Maraschino, and 1 measure orange juice. Shake vigorously until a frost forms, then strain into a chilled cocktail glass.

Bermuda Rose: put 4-6 cracked ice cubes into a cocktail shaker. Pour 2 measures gin, 2 teaspoons apricot brandy, 1 tablespoon lime juice, and 2 teaspoons grenadine over the ice. Shake vigorously until a frost forms. Fill a chilled glass with crushed ice. Strain the cocktail into the glass and top off with sparkling mineral water. Decorate with a lime slice.

Russian Rose: put 4–6 cracked ice cubes into a mixing glass. Dash orange bitters over the ice and pour in 3 measures strawberry-flavored vodka, ½ measure dry vermouth, and ½ measure grenadine. Stir gently to mix, then strain into a chilled cocktail glass.

English Rose: put 4–6 cracked ice cubes into a cocktail shaker. Dash lemon juice over the ice and pour in 2 measures gin, 2 measures dry vermouth, and 1 measure apricot brandy. Shake vigorously until a frost forms, then strain into a chilled cocktail glass.

Jack Rose: put 4–6 cracked ice cubes into a cocktail shaker. Add 2 measures applejack brandy or Calvados, ½ measure lime juice, and 1 teaspoon grenadine. Shake vigorously until a frost forms, then strain into a chilled cocktail glass.

Mint Julep

A julep is simply a mixed drink sweetened with syrup and it dates back to ancient times. The Mint Julep was probably first made in the United States, and it is the traditional drink of the Kentucky Derby.

serves 1

leaves of 1 fresh mint sprig

1 tbsp sugar syrup (see page 11)

6–8 crushed ice cubes

3 measures bourbon

fresh mint sprig, to decorate

❶ Put the mint leaves and sugar syrup into a small, chilled glass and mash with a teaspoon. Add the crushed ice to fill the glass, then add the bourbon.

❷ Decorate with the mint sprig.

Variations

Frozen Mint Julep: put 4–6 crushed ice cubes into a blender. Add 2 measures bourbon, 1 measure lemon juice, 1 measure sugar syrup (see page 11), and 6 fresh mint leaves. Process at low speed until slushy. Pour into a small, chilled glass and decorate with a fresh mint sprig.

Brandy Julep: fill a chilled glass with cracked ice. Add 2 measures brandy,

1 teaspoon sugar syrup (see page 11), and 4 fresh mint leaves. Stir well to mix and decorate with a fresh mint sprig and a lemon slice. Serve with a straw.

Jocose Julep: put 4–6 crushed ice cubes into a blender. Pour in 3 measures bourbon, 1 measure green crème de menthe, 1½ measures lime juice, and 1 teaspoon sugar syrup (see page 11). Add 5 fresh mint leaves. Process until smooth. Fill a chilled glass with cracked ice cubes and pour in the cocktail. Top off with sparkling mineral water and stir gently. Decorate with a fresh mint sprig.

Did you know?

The word "julep" is derived from Persian and came to us via Arabic. It means "rose water."

Whiskey Sour

Sours are short drinks, flavored with lemon or lime juice. They can be made with almost any spirit, although Whiskey Sour was the original.

serves 1

4–6 cracked ice cubes
2 measures American blended whiskey
1 measure lemon juice
1 tsp sugar syrup (see page 11)

To decorate
maraschino cherry
orange slice

❶ Put the cracked ice cubes into a cocktail shaker. Pour the whiskey, lemon juice, and sugar syrup over the ice. Shake vigorously until a frost forms.

❷ Strain into a chilled cocktail glass and decorate with the cherry speared on a toothpick and orange slice.

Variations

Bourbon Sour: substitute bourbon for the blended whiskey and decorate with an orange slice.

Brandy Sour: substitute 2½ measures brandy for the blended whiskey.

Boston Sour: to the ingredients in the cocktail shaker, add 1 egg white. Decorate with a maraschino cherry and a lemon slice.

Polynesian Sour: put 4–6 cracked ice cubes into a cocktail shaker and add 2 measures white rum, ½ measure lemon juice, ½ measure orange juice, and ½ measure guava juice. Shake until a frost forms, then pour into a chilled cocktail glass. Decorate with an orange slice.

Fireman's Sour: put 4–6 cracked ice cubes into a cocktail shaker and add 2 measures white rum, 1½ measures lime juice, 1 tablespoon grenadine, and 1 teaspoon sugar syrup (see page 11). Shake until a frost forms, then strain into a cocktail glass and decorate with a maraschino cherry and a lemon slice.

Strega Sour: put 4–6 cracked ice cubes into a cocktail shaker. Pour 2 measures gin, 1 measure Strega, and 1 measure lemon juice over the ice. Shake vigorously until a frost forms, then strain into a cocktail glass and decorate with a lemon slice.

Double Standard Sour: put 4–6 cracked ice cubes into a cocktail shaker and add 1½ measures blended whiskey, 1½ measures gin, 1 measure lemon juice, 1 teaspoon grenadine, and 1 teaspoon sugar syrup (see page 11). Shake until a frost forms, then strain into a chilled cocktail glass and decorate with a maraschino cherry and an orange slice.

Manhattan

Said to have been invented by Sir Winston Churchill's American mother, Jennie, the Manhattan is one of many cocktails named after places in New York City. The center of sophistication in the Jazz Age, the city is, once again, buzzing with cocktail bars for a new generation.

serves 1

4–6 cracked ice cubes
dash of Angostura bitters
3 measures rye whiskey
1 measure sweet vermouth
maraschino cherry, to decorate

❶ Put the cracked ice cubes into a mixing glass. Dash the Angostura bitters over the ice and pour in the whiskey and vermouth. Stir well to mix.

❷ Strain into a chilled glass and decorate with the maraschino cherry speared on a toothpick.

"City lights"

Harlem Cocktail: put 4–6 cracked ice cubes into a cocktail shaker. Pour 2 measures gin, 1½ measures pineapple juice, and 1 teaspoon Maraschino over the ice, and add 1 tablespoon chopped fresh pineapple. Shake vigorously until a frost forms, then strain into a small, chilled glass.

Brooklyn: put 4–6 cracked ice cubes into a mixing glass. Dash Amer Picon and Maraschino over the ice and pour in 2 measures rye whiskey and 1 measure dry vermouth. Stir to mix, then strain into a chilled cocktail glass.

Broadway Smile: pour 1 measure chilled triple sec into a small, chilled glass. With a steady hand, pour 1 measure chilled crème de cassis on top, without

mixing, then carefully pour 1 measure chilled Swedish Punsch on top, again without mixing.

Fifth Avenue: pour 1½ measures chilled dark crème de cacao into a small, chilled, straight-sided glass. With a steady hand, pour 1½ measures chilled apricot brandy on top, without mixing, then carefully pour ¾ measure chilled light cream on top, again without mixing.

Coney Island Baby: put 4–6 cracked ice cubes into a cocktail shaker. Pour 2 measures peppermint schnapps and 1 measure dark crème de cacao over the ice. Shake vigorously until a frost forms. Fill a small, chilled glass with cracked ice and strain the cocktail over it. Top off with soda water and stir gently.

Old Fashioned

So ubiquitous is this cocktail that a small, straight-sided glass is known as an Old Fashioned glass. It is a perfect illustration of the saying, "Sometimes the old ones are the best."

serves 1

sugar cube
dash of Angostura bitters
1 tsp water
2 measures bourbon or rye whiskey
4–6 cracked ice cubes
lemon peel twist, to decorate

❶ Put the sugar cube into a small, chilled Old Fashioned glass. Dash the Angostura bitters over the cube and add the water. Mash with a spoon until the sugar has dissolved.

❷ Pour the bourbon or rye whiskey into the glass and stir. Add the cracked ice cubes. Decorate with the lemon peel twist.

"Not old, but mellow"

Brandy Old Fashioned: put a sugar cube into a small, chilled glass. Dash Angostura bitters over the sugar to douse and add a dash of water. Mash with a spoon until the sugar has dissolved, then pour in 3 measures brandy and add 4–6 cracked ice cubes. Stir gently and decorate with a lemon peel twist.

Old Etonian: put 4–6 cracked ice cubes into a mixing glass. Dash crème de noyaux and orange bitters over the ice and pour in 1 measure gin and 1 measure Lillet. Stir, then strain into a chilled cocktail glass. Squeeze over a strip of orange peel.

Old Pal: put 4–6 cracked ice cubes into a cocktail shaker. Pour 2 measures rye whiskey, 1½ measures Campari, and 1 measure sweet vermouth over the ice. Shake vigorously until a frost forms, then strain into a chilled cocktail glass.

Old Trout: put 4–6 cracked ice cubes into a cocktail shaker. Pour 1 measure Campari and 2 measures orange juice over the ice. Shake vigorously until a frost forms. Fill a tall glass with ice cubes and strain the cocktail over them. Top off with sparkling mineral water and decorate with an orange slice.

Old Pale: put 4–6 cracked ice cubes into a mixing glass. Pour 2 measures bourbon, 1 measure Campari, and 1 measure dry vermouth over the ice. Stir well, then strain into a chilled cocktail glass. Squeeze over a strip of lemon peel.

Martini

For many, this is the ultimate cocktail. It is named for its inventor, Martini de Anna de Toggia, and not the famous brand of vermouth. The original version comprised equal measures of gin and vermouth, now known as a Fifty-Fifty, but the proportions vary, up to the Ultra Dry Martini, when the glass is merely rinsed out with vermouth before the gin is poured in.

serves 1

4–6 cracked ice cubes
3 measures gin
1 tsp dry vermouth, or to taste
cocktail olive, to decorate

❶ Put the cracked ice cubes into a mixing glass. Pour the gin and vermouth over the ice and stir well to mix.

❷ Strain into a chilled cocktail glass and decorate with the cocktail olive speared on a toothpick.

Variations

Gibson: decorate with 2–3 cocktail onions, instead of an olive.

Vodka Martini: substitute vodka for the gin.

Tequini: put 4–6 cracked ice cubes into a mixing glass. Dash Angostura bitters over the ice and pour in 3 measures white tequila and ½ measure dry vermouth. Stir well to mix. Strain into a chilled cocktail glass and decorate with a lemon peel twist.

Dirty Martini: put 4–6 cracked ice cubes into a cocktail shaker. Pour 3 measures gin, 1 measure dry vermouth, and ½ measure brine from a jar of cocktail olives over the ice. Shake vigorously until a frost forms, then strain into a chilled cocktail glass and decorate with a cocktail olive.

Saketini: put 4–6 cracked ice cubes into a cocktail shaker. Pour 3 measures gin and ½ measure sake over the ice. Shake vigorously until a frost forms, then strain into a chilled cocktail glass and decorate with a lemon peel twist.

Did you know?

Not only did James Bond always demand that his Martini should be shaken, not stirred, but his creator, Ian Fleming, also followed this practice.

Salty Dog

This is another cocktail that has changed since its invention. When it first appeared, gin-based cocktails were by far the most popular, but nowadays, a Salty Dog is more frequently made with vodka. You can use either spirit, but the cocktails will have different flavors.

serves 1

1 tbsp granulated sugar
1 tbsp coarse salt
lime wedge
6–8 cracked ice cubes
2 measures vodka
grapefruit juice, to top off

❶ Mix the sugar and salt together in a saucer. Rub the rim of a chilled Collins glass with the lime wedge, then dip it in the sugar and salt mixture to frost.
❷ Fill the glass with cracked ice cubes and pour the vodka over them. Top off with grapefruit juice and stir to mix. Serve with a straw.

Variations

Bride's Mother: put 4–6 cracked ice cubes into a cocktail shaker. Pour 1½ measures sloe gin, 1 measure gin, 2½ measures grapefruit juice, and ½ measure sugar syrup (see page 11) over the ice. Shake vigorously until a frost forms, then strain into a chilled cocktail glass.

AJ: put 4–6 cracked ice cubes into a cocktail shaker. Pour 1½ measures applejack or Calvados, and 1 measure grapefruit juice over the ice. Shake vigorously until a frost forms, then strain into a chilled cocktail glass.

Midnight Sun: put 4–6 cracked ice cubes into a cocktail shaker. Pour 2 measures aquavit, 1 measure grapefruit juice, and ¼ teaspoon grenadine over the ice. Shake vigorously until a frost forms, then strain into a chilled cocktail glass. Decorate with an orange slice.

Blinker: put 4–6 cracked ice cubes into a cocktail shaker. Pour 2 measures rye whiskey, 2½ measures grapefruit juice, and 1 teaspoon grenadine over the ice. Shake vigorously until a frost forms, then strain into a chilled cocktail glass.

Woodward: put 4–6 cracked ice cubes into a cocktail shaker. Pour 2 measures Scotch whisky, ½ measure dry vermouth, and ½ measure grapefruit juice over the ice. Shake vigorously until a frost forms, then strain the mixture into a chilled cocktail glass.

White Lady

Simple, elegant, subtle, and much more powerful than appearance suggests, this is the perfect cocktail to serve before an alfresco summer dinner.

serves 1

4–6 cracked ice cubes
2 measures gin
1 measure triple sec
1 measure lemon juice

❶ Put the cracked ice cubes into a cocktail shaker. Pour the gin, triple sec, and lemon juice over the ice. Shake vigorously until a frost forms.
❷ Strain into a chilled cocktail glass.

Variations

Green Lady: put 4–6 cracked ice cubes into a cocktail shaker. Dash lime juice over the ice and pour in 2 measures gin and 1 measure green Chartreuse. Shake vigorously until a frost forms, then strain into a chilled cocktail glass.

Creole Lady: put 4–6 cracked ice cubes into a mixing glass. Pour 2 measures bourbon, 1½ measures Madeira, and 1 teaspoon grenadine over the ice. Stir well to mix, then strain into a chilled cocktail glass. Decorate with maraschino cherries.

Perfect Lady: put 4–6 cracked ice cubes into a cocktail shaker. Pour 2 measures gin, 1 measure peach brandy, and 1 measure lemon juice over the ice. Add 1 teaspoon egg white. Shake until a frost forms, then strain into a chilled cocktail glass.

Apricot Lady: put 4–6 cracked ice cubes into a cocktail shaker. Pour 1½ measures white rum, 1 measure apricot brandy, 1 tablespoon lime juice, and ½ teaspoon triple sec over the ice, and add 1 egg white.

Shake vigorously until a frost forms. Half-fill a small, chilled glass with cracked ice. Strain the cocktail over the ice and decorate with an orange slice.

Blue Lady: put 4–6 cracked ice cubes into a cocktail shaker. Pour 2½ measures blue Curaçao, 1 measure white crème de cacao, and 1 measure light cream over the ice. Shake until a frost forms, then strain into a chilled cocktail glass.

My Fair Lady: put 4–6 cracked ice cubes into a cocktail shaker. Dash strawberry liqueur over the ice. Pour in 2 measures gin, 1 measure orange juice, and 1 measure lemon juice, and add 1 egg white. Shake vigorously until a frost forms, then strain into a chilled cocktail glass.

Shady Lady: put 4–6 cracked ice cubes into a cocktail shaker. Dash lime juice over the ice and pour in 3 measures tequila, 1 measure apple brandy, and 1 measure cranberry juice. Shake until a frost forms, then strain into a chilled cocktail glass.

Tom Collins

This cooling long drink combines gin, lemon juice, and soda water. This is a venerable cocktail, but the progenitor of several generations of the Collins family of drinks, scattered across the globe, was the John Collins cocktail.

serves 1

5–6 cracked ice cubes

3 measures gin

2 measures lemon juice

½ measure sugar syrup (see page 11)

soda water, to top off

lemon slice, to decorate

❶ Put the cracked ice cubes into a cocktail shaker. Pour the gin, lemon juice, and sugar syrup over the ice. Shake vigorously until a frost forms.

❷ Strain into a tall, chilled glass and top off with soda water. Decorate with a lemon slice.

Variations

John Collins: substitute Dutch gin or genever for the dry gin.

Mick Collins: substitute Irish whiskey for the gin.

Pierre Collins: substitute brandy for the gin.

Pedro Collins: substitute white rum for the gin.

Colonel Collins: substitute bourbon for the gin.

Mac Collins: substitute Scotch whisky for the gin.

Belle Collins: crush 2 fresh mint sprigs and place in a tall, chilled glass. Add 4–6 crushed ice cubes and pour in 2 measures gin, 1 measure lemon juice, and 1 teaspoon sugar syrup (see page 11).

Top off with sparkling water, stir gently, and decorate with a fresh mint sprig.

Juan Collins: half-fill a chilled glass with cracked ice cubes and pour in 2 measures white tequila, 1 measure lemon juice, and 1 teaspoon sugar syrup (see page 11). Top off with sparkling water and stir gently. Decorate with a maraschino cherry.

Country Cousin Collins: put 4–6 crushed ice cubes into a blender or food processor. Dash orange bitters over the ice. Add 2 measures apple brandy, 1 measure lemon juice, and ½ teaspoon sugar syrup (see page 11). Blend at medium speed for 10 seconds. Pour into a tall, chilled glass. Top off with sparkling water. Stir and decorate with a lemon slice.

Singapore Sling

In the days of the British Empire, the privileged would gather in the relative cool of the evening at exclusive clubs to refresh parched throats and gossip about the day's events. Those days are long gone, but a Singapore Sling is still the ideal thirst-quencher on hot evenings.

serves 1

10–12 cracked ice cubes
2 measures gin
1 measure cherry brandy
1 measure lemon juice
1 tsp grenadine
soda water, to top off

To decorate
lime peel strip
maraschino cherries

❶ Put 4–6 cracked ice cubes into a cocktail shaker. Pour the gin, cherry brandy, lemon juice, and grenadine over the ice. Shake vigorously until a frost forms.

❷ Half-fill a chilled highball glass with cracked ice cubes and strain the cocktail over them. Top off with soda water and then decorate with the lime peel strip and maraschino cherries speared on a toothpick.

Variations

Sweet Singapore Sling: put 4–6 cracked ice cubes into a cocktail shaker. Dash lemon juice over the ice and pour in 1 measure gin and 2 measures cherry brandy. Shake vigorously until a frost forms. Half-fill a chilled glass with cracked ice cubes and strain the cocktail over them. Top off with soda water and decorate with maraschino cherries.

Gin Sling: put 1 teaspoon sugar in a mixing glass. Add 1 measure lemon juice and 1 teaspoon water and stir until the sugar has dissolved. Pour in 2 measures gin and stir to mix. Half-fill a small, chilled glass with ice and strain the cocktail over it. Decorate with an orange peel twist.

Whiskey Sling: put 1 teaspoon sugar in a mixing glass. Add 1 measure lemon juice and 1 teaspoon water and stir until the sugar has dissolved. Pour in 2 measures American blended whiskey and stir to mix. Half-fill a small, chilled glass with ice and strain the cocktail over it. Decorate with an orange peel twist.

Long Island Iced Tea

Like many other classics, this cocktail dates from the days of Prohibition, when it was drunk from tea cups in an unconvincing attempt to fool the FBI that it was a harmless beverage. It started out life as a simple combination of vodka colored with a dash of cola, but has evolved into a more elaborate, but no less potent, concoction.

serves 1

10–12 cracked ice cubes

2 measures vodka

1 measure gin

1 measure white tequila

1 measure white rum

½ measure white crème de menthe

2 measures lemon juice

1 tsp sugar syrup (see page 11)

cola, to top off

lime or lemon wedge, to decorate

❶ Put 4–6 cracked ice cubes into a cocktail shaker. Pour the vodka, gin, tequila, rum, crème de menthe, lemon juice, and sugar syrup over the ice. Shake vigorously until a frost forms.

❷ Half-fill a tall, chilled Collins glass with cracked ice cubes and strain the cocktail over them. Top off with cola and decorate with the lime or lemon wedge.

"Brewing up"

Artillery Punch (serves 30): pour 4 cups bourbon, 4 cups red wine, 4 cups strong, black tea, 2 cups dark rum, 1 cup gin, 1 cup apricot brandy, 4 measures lemon juice, 4 measures lime juice, and 4 tablespoons sugar syrup (see page 11) into a large bowl. Let chill for 2 hours. To serve, place a large block of ice into a punch bowl. Pour the punch over the ice and decorate with thinly sliced lemon and lime.

Did you know?

In 1920, there were about 15,000 bars in New York. Following the introduction of Prohibition in 1920, the number of illegal speakeasies rocketed to about 32,000.

Piña Colada

One of the younger generation of classics, this became popular during the cocktail revival of the 1980s and has remained so ever since.

serves 1

4–6 crushed ice cubes
2 measures white rum
1 measure dark rum
3 measures pineapple juice
2 measures coconut cream
fresh pineapple wedges, to decorate

❶ Put the crushed ice into a blender or food processor and add the white rum, dark rum, pineapple juice, and coconut cream. Blend until smooth.

❷ Pour, without straining, into a tall, chilled glass and decorate with pineapple wedges speared on a toothpick.

Variations

Lighten Up Piña Colada: put 4–6 cracked ice cubes into a cocktail shaker. Pour 2 measures white rum, 2 measures Malibu, and 3 measures pineapple juice over the ice. Shake vigorously until a frost forms. Half-fill a small, chilled glass with cracked ice cubes. Strain the cocktail over them. Decorate with a pineapple slice.

Amigos Piña Colada (to serve 4): put 10–12 crushed ice cubes into a blender or food processor and add 1 cup white rum, 1¼ cups pineapple juice, 5 measures coconut cream, 2 measures dark rum, and 2 measures light cream. Blend until smooth. Pour, without straining, into long, chilled glasses and decorate with pineapple wedges speared on toothpicks.

Strawberry Colada: put 4–6 crushed ice cubes into a blender or food processor and add 3 measures golden rum, 4 measures pineapple juice, 1 measure coconut cream, and 6 hulled fresh strawberries. Blend until smooth. Pour, without straining, into a tall, chilled glass. Decorate with fresh pineapple wedges and strawberries speared on a toothpick.

Banana Colada: put 4–6 crushed ice cubes into a blender or food processor and add 2 measures white rum, 4 measures pineapple juice, 1 measure Malibu, and 1 peeled and sliced banana. Blend until smooth. Pour, without straining, into a tall, chilled glass and serve with a straw.

Acapulco

This is one of many cocktails that has changed from its original recipe over the years. To begin with, it was always rum-based and did not include any fruit juice. Nowadays, it is increasingly made with tequila, because this has become better known outside its native Mexico.

serves 1

10–12 cracked ice cubes
2 measures white rum
½ measure triple sec
½ measure lime juice
1 tsp sugar syrup (see page 11)
1 egg white
fresh mint sprig, to decorate

❶ Put 4–6 cracked ice cubes into a cocktail shaker. Pour the rum, triple sec, lime juice, and sugar syrup over the ice, and add the egg white. Shake vigorously until a frost forms.

❷ Half-fill a chilled highball glass with cracked ice cubes and strain the cocktail over them. Decorate with the mint sprig.

Variations

Tequila Acapulco: put 4–6 cracked ice cubes into a cocktail shaker. Pour 1 measure white tequila, 1 measure white rum, 4 measures pineapple juice, and 1 measure lime juice over the ice. Shake vigorously until a frost forms. Half-fill a small, chilled glass with cracked ice cubes and strain the cocktail over them.

Acapulco Gold: put 4–6 cracked ice cubes into a cocktail shaker and add 1 measure golden tequila, 1 measure golden rum, 2 measures pineapple juice, 1 measure coconut cream, and 1 measure grapefruit juice. Shake until a frost forms. Half-fill a chilled glass with cracked ice cubes and strain the cocktail over them.

Did you know?

Rum owes its origin to Christopher Columbus, who is said to have planted the first sugar cane on the islands of the Caribbean.

Daiquiri

Daiquiri is a town in Cuba, where this drink was said to have been invented in the early part of the 20th century. A businessman had run out of imported gin, so he had to make do with the local drink—rum—which, at that time, was of unreliable quality. To ensure that his guests would find it palatable, he decided to mix it with other ingredients. This classic has since given rise to almost innumerable variations.

serves 1

4–6 cracked ice cubes
2 measures white rum
³/₄ measure lime juice
½ tsp sugar syrup (see page 11)

❶ Put the cracked ice cubes into a cocktail shaker. Pour the rum, lime juice, and sugar syrup over the ice. Shake vigorously until a frost forms.
❷ Strain into a chilled cocktail glass.

Variations

Derby Daiquiri: put 4–6 crushed ice cubes into a blender or food processor and add 2 measures white rum, 1 measure orange juice, ½ measure triple sec, and ½ measure lime juice. Blend until smooth. Pour, without straining, into a chilled cocktail glass.

Banana Daiquiri: put 4–6 crushed ice cubes into a blender or food processor and then add 2 measures white rum, ½ measure triple sec, ½ measure lime juice, ½ measure light cream, 1 teaspoon sugar syrup (see page 11), and ¼ peeled and sliced banana. Blend until smooth. Pour the mixture, without straining, into a chilled goblet and decorate it with a lime slice.

Peach Daiquiri: put 4–6 crushed ice cubes into a blender or food processor and add 2 measures white rum, 1 measure lime juice, ½ teaspoon sugar syrup (see page 11), and ½ peeled and chopped peach. Blend until smooth. Pour, without straining, into a chilled goblet.

Passionate Daiquiri: put 4–6 cracked ice cubes into a cocktail shaker. Pour 2 measures white rum, 1 measure lime juice, and ½ measure passion fruit syrup over the ice. Shake vigorously until a frost forms. Strain into a chilled cocktail glass and decorate with a maraschino cherry.

Bartender's Tip
For other Daiquiri variations, see page 70.

Cuba Libre

The 1960s and 1970s saw the meteoric rise in popularity of this simple, long drink, perhaps because of successful marketing by Bacardi brand rum—the original white Cuban rum (now produced in the Bahamas)—and Coca-Cola, but more likely because rum and cola seem to be natural companions.

serves 1

4–6 cracked ice cubes
2 measures white rum
cola, to top off
lime wedge, to decorate

❶ Half-fill a glass with cracked ice cubes. Pour the rum over the ice and top off with cola.

❷ Stir gently to mix and decorate with a lime wedge.

Other Cuban classics

Bacardi Cocktail: put 4–6 cracked ice cubes into a cocktail shaker. Pour 2 measures Bacardi rum, 1 measure grenadine, and 1 measure fresh lime juice over the ice. Shake vigorously until a frost forms. Strain into a chilled cocktail glass.

Brandy Cuban: half-fill a chilled glass with cracked ice cubes. Pour 1½ measures brandy and ½ measure lime juice over the ice. Top off with cola and stir gently. Decorate with a lime slice.

Cuban: put 4–6 cracked ice cubes into a cocktail shaker. Pour 2 measures brandy, 1 measure apricot brandy, 1 measure lime juice, and 1 teaspoon white rum over the ice. Shake vigorously until a frost forms. Strain into a chilled cocktail glass.

Cuban Special: put 4–6 cracked ice cubes into a cocktail shaker. Pour 2 measures rum, 1 measure lime juice, 1 tablespoon pineapple juice, and 1 teaspoon triple sec over the ice. Shake vigorously until a frost forms. Strain into a chilled cocktail glass and decorate with a fresh pineapple wedge.

Did you know?

Britain's Royal Navy continued to provide sailors with a daily rum ration until 1969, although, by then, the quantity had been reduced from the original 1¼ cups.

Zombie

The individual ingredients of this cocktail, including liqueurs and fruit juices, vary considerably from one recipe to another, but all zombies contain a mixture of white, golden, and dark rum in a range of proportions.

serves 1

4–6 crushed ice cubes

2 measures dark rum

2 measures white rum

1 measure golden rum

1 measure triple sec

1 measure lime juice

1 measure orange juice

1 measure pineapple juice

1 measure guava juice

1 tbsp grenadine

1 tbsp orgeat

1 tsp Pernod

To decorate

fresh mint sprig

pineapple wedges

maraschino cherries

❶ Put the crushed ice into a blender or food processor and add the three rums, triple sec, lime juice, orange juice, pineapple juice, guava juice, grenadine, orgeat, and Pernod. Blend until smooth.

❷ Pour, without straining, into a chilled Collins glass and decorate with the mint sprig, and the pineapple wedges and maraschino cherries speared on a toothpick.

Variations

Walking Zombie: put 4–6 cracked ice cubes into a cocktail shaker. Pour 1 measure white rum, 1 measure golden rum, 1 measure dark rum, 1 measure apricot brandy, 1 measure lime juice, 1 measure pineapple juice, and 1 teaspoon sugar syrup (see page 11) over the ice. Shake vigorously until a frost forms. Half-fill a chilled glass with cracked ice cubes and strain the cocktail over them. Decorate with orange and lemon slices.
Zombie Prince: put 4–6 cracked ice cubes into a mixing glass. Dash Angostura bitters over the ice, then pour in 1 measure white rum, 1 measure golden rum, 1 measure dark rum, ½ measure lemon juice, ½ measure orange juice, and ½ measure grapefruit juice and add 1 teaspoon brown sugar. Stir to mix well, then strain into a tall, chilled tumbler.

Bartender's Tip
Orgeat is an almond-flavored syrup. If you can't find it, you could substitute the same amount of Amaretto, which is more widely available.

Mai Tai

For some reason, this cocktail always inspires elaborate decoration with paper parasols, a selection of fruit, and spirals of citrus peel—sometimes so much so that you can be in danger of stabbing your nose on a toothpick when you try to drink it. If you want to go wild with decorations—and why not—serve the drink with one or two long, colorful straws.

serves 1

4–6 cracked ice cubes
2 measures white rum
2 measures dark rum
1 measure clear Curaçao
1 measure lime juice
1 tbsp orgeat
1 tbsp grenadine

To decorate
pineapple wedges
maraschino cherries
orchid (optional)
paper parasol (optional)

❶ Put the cracked ice cubes into a cocktail shaker. Pour the white and dark rums, Curaçao, lime juice, orgeat, and grenadine over the ice. Shake vigorously until a frost forms.

❷ Strain into a chilled Collins glass and decorate with the pineapple wedges and cherries speared on a toothpick, adding an orchid and paper parasol, if desired.

Other decorated cocktails

Generally speaking, you can decorate cocktails in any way you like—or not at all, if you prefer. There are some, however, that are traditionally served in a particular way. The Martini and the Gibson (see page 30), for example, are differentiated only because the former is decorated with a cocktail olive, while the latter is always served with a "cocktail onion."

Horse's Neck: hang a long spiral of lemon peel over the rim of a tall, chilled glass. Fill the glass with cracked ice and pour 2 measures American blended whiskey over the ice. Top off with ginger ale and stir.

Ultimate Beefeater Martini: put 4–6 cracked ice cubes into a mixing glass. Dash dry vermouth over the ice and pour in 1 measure Beefeater gin. Stir well to mix and strain the mixture into a chilled cocktail glass. Decorate with a sliver of fillet steak.

Margarita

The traditional way to drink tequila is to shake a little salt on the back of your hand between the thumb and forefinger and, holding a wedge of lime or lemon, lick the salt, suck the fruit, and then down a shot of tequila in one. This cocktail, attributed to Francisco Morales and invented in 1942 in Mexico, is a more civilized version.

serves 1

lime wedge
coarse salt
4–6 cracked ice cubes
3 measures white tequila
1 measure triple sec
2 measures lime juice
lime slice, to decorate

❶ Rub the rim of a chilled cocktail glass with the lime wedge and then dip in a saucer of coarse salt to frost.
❷ Put the cracked ice cubes into a cocktail shaker. Pour the tequila, triple sec, and lime juice over the ice. Shake vigorously until a frost forms.
❸ Strain into the prepared glass and decorate with the lime slice.

Variations

Frozen Margarita: put 6–8 cracked ice cubes into a blender or food processor and add 2 measures white tequila, 1 measure lime juice, and ½ measure triple sec. Blend at low speed until slushy. Pour, without straining, into a chilled cocktail glass and decorate with a lime slice.

Blue Margarita: frost the rim of a chilled cocktail glass using a lime wedge and coarse salt (as above). Put 4–6 cracked ice cubes into a cocktail shaker. Pour 2 measures white tequila, 1 measure blue Curaçao, 1½ measures lime juice, and 1 tablespoon triple sec over the ice. Shake vigorously until a frost forms. Strain into the prepared glass and decorate with a lime slice.

Margarita Impériale: put 4–6 cracked ice cubes into a cocktail shaker. Dash clear Curaçao over the ice and pour in 1 measure white tequila, 1 measure Mandarine Napoléon, and 1 measure lemon juice. Shake vigorously until a frost forms. Strain into a chilled cocktail glass.

Peach Margarita: frost the rim of a chilled cocktail glass using a lime wedge and coarse salt (as above). Put 4–6 cracked ice cubes into a cocktail shaker. Pour 2 measures white tequila, 2 measures lime juice, ½ measure peach liqueur, and 1 tablespoon triple sec over the ice. Shake vigorously until a frost forms. Strain into the prepared glass and decorate with a fresh peach slice.

Tequila Sunrise

You shouldn't rush when making this cocktail, otherwise you will spoil the sunrise effect as the grenadine slowly spreads through the orange juice.

serves 1

4–6 cracked ice cubes
2 parts white tequila
orange juice, to top off
1 measure grenadine

❶ Put the cracked ice cubes into a chilled highball glass. Pour the tequila over the ice and top off with the orange juice. Stir well to mix.

❷ Slowly pour in the grenadine and serve with a straw.

Variations

Blinding Sunrise: put 4–6 cracked ice cubes into a cocktail shaker. Pour 1 measure white tequila, 1 measure vodka, 3 measures orange juice, and 1 teaspoon triple sec over the ice. Shake until a frost forms. Half-fill a glass with cracked ice cubes and strain the cocktail over them. Slowly pour in 1 measure grenadine.

Pacific Sunrise: put 4–6 cracked ice cubes into a cocktail shaker. Dash Angostura bitters over the ice and pour in 1 measure white tequila, 1 measure blue Curaçao, and 1 measure lime juice. Shake vigorously until a frost forms, then strain into a chilled cocktail glass.

Mint Sunrise: put 4–6 cracked ice cubes into a chilled glass. Pour 1½ measures Scotch whisky, ½ measure brandy, and ½ measure clear Curaçao over the ice and stir gently. Decorate with a fresh mint sprig and a lemon slice.

Did you know?

The popularity of tequila took producers by surprise. The agave plant from which it is made takes 8–10 years to mature: slow maturation and cultivation problems created a severe shortage by the year 2000, which resulted in rocketing prices and a lucrative trade in "cactus rustling."

Bloody Mary

This classic cocktail was invented in 1921 at the legendary Harry's Bar in Paris. There are numerous versions—some much hotter and spicier than others. Ingredients may include horseradish sauce in addition to or instead of Tabasco sauce, more or less tomato juice, and lime juice instead of lemon. Sometimes the glass is decorated with a sprig of mint. Whatever the version, all experts agree that it is essential to use the highest-quality ingredients.

serves 1

4–6 cracked ice cubes

dash of Worcestershire sauce

dash of Tabasco sauce

2 measures vodka

6 measures tomato juice

juice of ½ lemon

pinch of celery salt

pinch of cayenne pepper

To decorate

celery stalk with leaves

lemon slice

❶ Put the cracked ice cubes into a cocktail shaker. Dash the Worcestershire sauce and Tabasco sauce over the ice and pour in the vodka, tomato juice, and lemon juice. Shake vigorously until a frost forms.

❷ Strain into a chilled glass, add a pinch of celery salt and a pinch of cayenne, and decorate with the celery stalk and the lemon slice.

Variations

Bloody Maria: substitute 2 measures white tequila for the vodka, then add 1 teaspoon horseradish sauce and a pinch of ground coriander. Decorate with a lime wedge.

Cold and Clammy Bloody Mary: substitute 3 measures clam juice for 3 of the measures of tomato juice and decorate with a scallion curl.

Bullshot: substitute 4 measures chilled beef bouillon for the tomato juice. Season to taste with salt and pepper.

Moscow Mule

This cocktail came into existence through a happy coincidence during the 1930s. An American bar owner had overstocked ginger beer, and a representative of a soda company invented this drink to help him out.

serves 1

10–12 cracked ice cubes
2 measures vodka
1 measure lime juice
ginger beer, to top off
lime slice, to decorate

❶ Put 4–6 cracked ice cubes into a cocktail shaker. Pour the vodka and lime juice over the ice. Shake vigorously until a frost forms.

❷ Half-fill a chilled highball glass with cracked ice cubes and strain the cocktail over them. Top off with ginger beer and decorate with the lime slice.

Other stubborn drinks

Delft Donkey: make a Moscow Mule, but substitute gin for the vodka.

Mississippi Mule: put 4–6 cracked ice cubes into a cocktail shaker. Pour 2 measures gin, ½ measure crème de cassis, and ½ measure lemon juice over the ice. Shake vigorously until a frost forms, then strain into a small, chilled glass.

Mule's Hind Leg: put 4–6 cracked ice cubes into a cocktail shaker. Pour in ½ measure apricot brandy, ½ measure apple brandy, ½ measure Bénédictine, ½ measure gin, and ½ measure maple syrup. Shake vigorously until a frost forms, then strain into a chilled cocktail glass.

Jamaica Mule: put 4–6 cracked ice cubes into a cocktail shaker. Pour 2 measures white rum, 1 measure dark rum, 1 measure golden rum, 1 measure Falernum, and 1 measure lime juice over the ice. Shake vigorously until a frost forms, then strain the mixture into a tall, chilled glass. Top off with ginger beer and decorate with some fresh pineapple wedges and pieces of candied ginger.

Bartender's Tip

Falernum is a Caribbean syrup used in rum drinks. It is flavored with lime juice, almonds, ginger, and spices.

Screwdriver

Always use freshly squeezed orange juice to make this refreshing cocktail—it is just not the same with bottled juice. This simple, classic cocktail has given rise to numerous and increasingly elaborate variations.

serves 1

6–8 cracked ice cubes
2 measures vodka
orange juice, to top up
orange slice, to decorate

❶ Fill a chilled glass with cracked ice cubes. Pour the vodka over the ice and top up with orange juice.

❷ Stir well to mix and decorate with the orange slice.

Variations

Cordless Screwdriver: pour 2 measures chilled vodka into a shot glass. Dip a wedge of orange into superfine sugar. Down the vodka in one go and suck the orange.

Creamy Screwdriver: put 4–6 crushed ice cubes into a blender or food processor. Add 2 measures vodka, 6 measures orange juice, 1 egg yolk, and ½ teaspoon sugar syrup (see page 11). Blend until smooth. Half-fill a chilled glass with cracked ice cubes and pour the cocktail over them without straining.

Harvey Wallbanger: make a Screwdriver and then float 1 measure Galliano on top by pouring it gently over the back of a teaspoon.

Slow Screw: substitute sloe gin for the vodka.

Bartender's Tip

Galliano is a honey- and vanilla-flavored liqueur from Italy. It is sold in tall, thin bottles, so bars store it on a top shelf up against the wall to avoid knocking it over.

Did you know?

The Harvey Wallbanger is named for the Californian surfer who took such prodigious delight in drinking Screwdrivers topped with a Galliano float that he ricocheted from wall to wall on leaving the bar.

Kir

As with the best mustard, crème de cassis production is centered on the French city of Dijon. This cocktail is named in commemoration of a partisan and mayor of the city, Félix Kir.

serves 1

4–6 cracked ice cubes
2 measures crème de cassis
white wine, to top off
lemon peel twist, to decorate

❶ Put the cracked ice cubes into a chilled wine glass. Pour the crème de cassis over the ice.

❷ Top off with chilled white wine and stir well. Decorate with the lemon peel twist.

Wine toppers

Kir Royale: substitute champagne for the white wine.

Osborne (named for Queen Victoria's Isle of Wight residence and apparently a favorite tipple of Her Majesty's): pour 3 measures claret and 1 measure Scotch whisky into a goblet and stir to mix.

Bellini (created at Harry's Bar, Venice, and named after the Renaissance artist): fill a goblet with crushed ice and dash over grenadine. Pour in 1 measure peach juice, then top off with chilled champagne. Decorate with a peeled, fresh peach slice.

Bellinitini: put 4–6 cracked ice cubes into a cocktail shaker. Pour in 2 measures vodka, 1 measure peach schnapps, and 1 measure peach juice. Shake until a frost forms, then strain into a chilled goblet. Top off with chilled champagne.

Rikki-Tikki-Tavi: put a sugar cube into a chilled champagne flute and dash with Angostura bitters until red but still intact. Pour in 1 teaspoon brandy and 1 teaspoon clear Curaçao and top off with chilled champagne.

Champagne Pick-me-up: put 4–6 cracked ice cubes into a cocktail shaker. Dash grenadine over the ice and pour in 2 measures brandy, 1 measure orange juice, and 1 measure lemon juice. Shake vigorously until a frost forms. Strain into a wine glass and top off with chilled champagne.

Buck's Fizz

Invented at Buck's Club in London, the original was invariably made with Bollinger champagne and it is true that the better the quality of the champagne, the better the flavor.

serves 1

2 measures chilled champagne
2 measures chilled orange juice

❶ Pour the champagne into a chilled champagne flute, then pour in the orange juice.

Variations

Duck's Fizz: substitute Canard-Duchêne champagne for the Bollinger.

Mimosa: pour the orange juice into the flute and then the champagne. Stir gently. You can use sparkling white wine instead of champagne.

Black Velvet: pour 1¼ cups chilled champagne or sparkling wine and 1¼ cups chilled stout into a chilled glass at the same time. Do not stir.

Soyer au Champagne: put 1 scoop vanilla ice cream into a wine glass and add ¼ teaspoon brandy, ¼ teaspoon triple sec,

and ¼ teaspoon Maraschino. Stir to mix, then top off with chilled champagne. Stir, then decorate with a maraschino cherry.

Champagne Cup: pour ½ measure brandy and ½ measure clear Curaçao into a chilled wine glass. Add 1 ice cube and top off with champagne. Decorate with a sprig of fresh mint and an orange slice.

Spritzer: fill a wine glass with cracked ice cubes and pour in 3 measures white wine. Top off with soda water or sparkling mineral water and decorate with a lemon peel twist.

Did you know?

In spite of his ruthless ambition and Prussian earnestness, Otto von Bismarck must have had a more frivolous side to his nature because he is reputed to have created the Black Velvet.

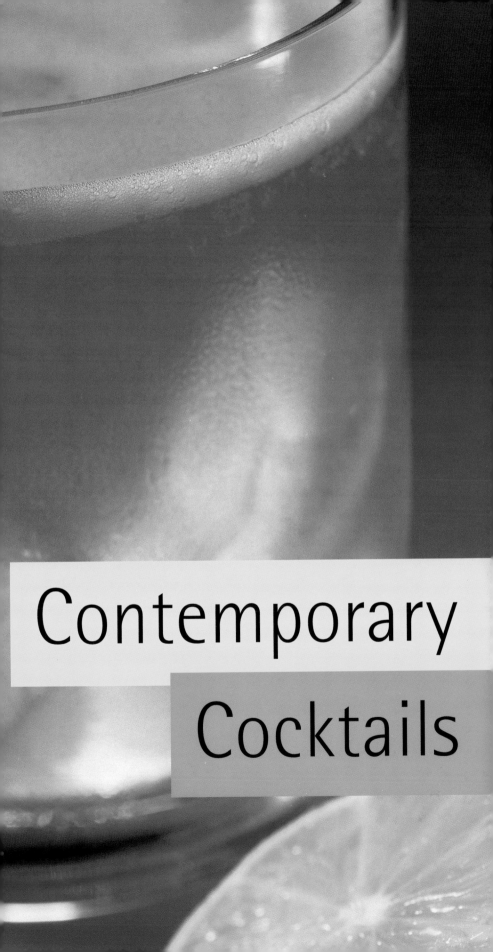

Contemporary
Cocktails

Frozen Daiquiri

One of the great classic cocktails, the Daiquiri (see page 46) has moved on. It's not just mixed with fresh fruit or unusual ingredients, it's entered the 21st century with a whole new future, as slushes take on a leading role in fashionable cocktail bars.

serves 1

6 crushed ice cubes

2 measures white rum

1 measure lime juice

1 tsp sugar syrup (see page 11)

lime slice, to decorate

❶ Put the crushed ice into a blender or food processor and add the rum, lime juice, and sugar syrup. Blend until slushy.

❷ Pour into a chilled champagne flute and decorate with the lime slice.

Variations

Frozen Pineapple Daiquiri: put 6 crushed ice cubes into a blender or food processor and add 2 measures white rum, 1 measure lime juice, ½ teaspoon pineapple syrup, and ½ cup finely chopped fresh pineapple. Blend until slushy. Pour into a chilled cocktail glass. Decorate with fresh pineapple wedges.

Frozen Mint Daiquiri: put 6 crushed ice cubes into a blender or food processor and add 2 measures white rum, ½ measure lime juice, 1 teaspoon sugar syrup (see page 11), and 6 fresh mint leaves. Blend until slushy. Pour into a chilled cocktail glass.

Frozen Strawberry Daiquiri: put 6 crushed ice cubes into a blender or food processor and add 2 measures white rum, 1 measure lime juice, 1 teaspoon sugar syrup (see page 11), and 6 fresh or frozen strawberries. Blend until slushy. Pour into a chilled glass. Decorate with a strawberry.

Frozen Peach Daiquiri: put 6 crushed ice cubes into a blender or food processor and add 2 measures white rum, 1 measure lime juice, 1 teaspoon sugar syrup (see page 11), and ½ peeled and finely chopped peach. Blend until slushy. Pour into a chilled cocktail glass. Decorate with a fresh peach slice.

Tequila Slammer

Slammers, also known as shooters, are currently very fashionable. The idea is that you pour the different ingredients directly into the glass, normally without stirring (some slammers form colorful layers). Cover the top of the glass with one hand to prevent spillage, then slam the glass on the bar or a table to mix, and drink the cocktail down in one. It is essential to use a strong glass that is unlikely to break under such treatment.

serves 1

1 measure white tequila
1 measure lemon juice
chilled sparkling wine, to top off

❶ Put the tequila and lemon juice into a chilled glass and stir to mix. Top off with sparkling wine.
❷ Cover the glass with your hand and slam.

"Those little shooters, how I love to drink them down..."

Alabama Slammer: put 4–6 cracked ice cubes into a mixing glass. Pour 1 measure Southern Comfort, 1 measure Amaretto, and ½ measure sloe gin over the ice and stir to mix. Strain into a shot glass and add ½ teaspoon lemon juice. Cover and slam.

B52: pour 1 measure chilled dark crème de cacao into a shot glass. With a steady hand, gently pour in 1 measure chilled Bailey's Irish Cream to make a second layer, then gently pour in 1 measure chilled Grand Marnier. Cover and slam.

B52 (second version): pour 1 measure chilled Kahlúa into a shot glass. With a steady hand, gently pour in 1 measure chilled Bailey's Irish Cream to make a second layer, then gently pour in 1 measure chilled Grand Marnier. Cover and slam.

Banana Slip: pour 1 measure chilled crème de banane into a shot glass. With a steady hand, gently pour in 1 measure chilled Bailey's Irish Cream to make a second layer. Cover and slam.

Wild Night Out

Tequila has a reputation for being an extraordinarily potent spirit, but most commercially exported brands are the same standard strength as other spirits, such as gin or whiskey. "Home-grown" tequila or its close relative, mescal, may be another matter.

serves 1

10–12 cracked ice cubes
3 measures white tequila
2 measures cranberry juice
1 measure lime juice
soda water, to top off

❶ Put 4–6 cracked ice cubes into a cocktail shaker. Pour the tequila, cranberry juice, and lime juice over the ice. Shake vigorously until a frost forms.
❷ Half-fill a chilled glass with cracked ice cubes and strain the cocktail over them. Add soda water to taste.

The wild bunch

Buttafuoco: put 4–6 cracked ice cubes into a cocktail shaker. Pour 2 measures white tequila, ½ measure Galliano, ½ measure cherry brandy, and ½ measure lemon juice over the ice. Shake vigorously until a frost forms. Half-fill a glass with cracked ice cubes and strain the cocktail over them. Top off with soda water and decorate with a maraschino cherry.

Magna Carta: rub the rim of a wine glass with a wedge of lime, then dip in a saucer of superfine sugar to frost. Put 4–6 cracked ice cubes into a mixing glass. Pour 2 measures white tequila and 1 measure triple sec over the ice and stir well to mix.

Strain into the prepared glass and top off with chilled sparkling wine.

Tequila Fizz: put 4–6 cracked ice cubes into a cocktail shaker. Pour 3 measures white tequila, 1 measure grenadine, and 1 measure lime juice over the ice and add 1 egg white. Shake vigorously until a frost forms. Half-fill a chilled glass with cracked ice cubes and strain the cocktail over them. Top off with ginger ale.

Changuirongo: half-fill a tall, chilled glass with cracked ice cubes. Pour 2 measures white tequila over the ice and top off with ginger ale. Stir gently and decorate with a lime slice.

Carolina

White tequila is most commonly used for mixing cocktails, but some require the mellower flavor of the amber-colored, aged tequilas, which are known as golden tequila or añejo.

serves 1

4–6 cracked ice cubes
3 measures golden tequila
1 tsp grenadine
1 tsp vanilla extract
1 measure light cream
1 egg white

To decorate
ground cinnamon
maraschino cherry

❶ Put the cracked ice cubes into a cocktail shaker. Pour the tequila, grenadine, vanilla extract, and cream over the ice and add the egg white. Shake vigorously until a frost forms.
❷ Strain into a chilled cocktail glass. Sprinkle with cinnamon and decorate with the maraschino cherry.

The golden touch

Grapeshot: put 4–6 cracked ice cubes into a cocktail shaker. Pour 2 measures golden tequila, 1 measure clear Curaçao, and 1½ measures white grape juice over the ice and shake vigorously until a frost forms. Strain into a chilled cocktail glass.

Chapala: put 4–6 cracked ice cubes into a cocktail shaker. Pour 2 measures golden tequila, 2 measures orange juice, 1 measure lime juice, ½ measure triple sec, and ½ measure grenadine over the ice. Shake vigorously until a frost forms. Half-fill a chilled glass with cracked ice cubes and strain the cocktail over them.

Piñata: put 4–6 cracked ice cubes into a cocktail shaker and add 2 measures golden tequila, 1 measure crème de banane, and 1½ measures lime juice. Shake until a frost forms. Strain into a chilled glass.

Montezuma: put 4–6 crushed ice cubes into a blender or food processor and add 2 measures golden tequila, 1 measure Madeira, and 1 egg yolk. Blend until smooth. Pour into a chilled cocktail glass.

Crocodile

This is certainly a snappy cocktail with a bit of bite. However, it probably gets its name from its spectacular color created by the addition of Midori, a Japanese melon-flavored liqueur, which is a startling shade of green.

serves 1

4–6 cracked ice cubes

2 measures vodka

1 measure triple sec

1 measure Midori

2 measures lemon juice

❶ Put the cracked ice cubes into a cocktail shaker. Pour the vodka, triple sec, Midori, and lemon juice over the ice. Shake vigorously until a frost forms.
❷ Strain into a chilled cocktail glass.

Variations

Alligator: put 4–6 cracked ice cubes into a cocktail shaker. Pour 2 measures vodka, 1 measure Midori, 1/2 measure dry vermouth, and 1/4 teaspoon lemon juice over the ice. Shake vigorously until a frost forms. Strain into a chilled cocktail glass.

Melon Ball: put 4–6 cracked ice cubes into a mixing glass. Pour 2 measures vodka, 2 measures Midori, and 4 measures pineapple juice over the ice and stir well to mix. Half-fill a chilled glass with cracked ice cubes and strain the cocktail over them. Decorate with a melon wedge.

Melon Balls: put 4–6 cracked ice cubes into a cocktail shaker. Pour 1 measure vodka, 1 measure Midori, and 1 measure pineapple juice over the ice. Shake vigorously until a frost forms, then strain into a chilled cocktail glass.

Melon State Balls: put 4–6 cracked ice cubes into a cocktail shaker. Pour 2 measures vodka, 1 measure Midori, and 2 measures orange juice over the ice. Shake vigorously until a frost forms, then strain the mixture into a chilled cocktail glass.

Vodga

As a rule, classic cocktails based on vodka were intended to provide the kick of an alcoholic drink with no tell-tale signs on the breath, and they were usually simple mixes of fruit juice, sodas, and other nonalcoholic flavorings. By contrast, contemporary cocktails based on vodka often include other aromatic and flavorsome ingredients, with vodka adding extra strength.

serves 1

4–6 cracked ice cubes

2 measures vodka

1 measure Strega

½ measure orange juice

❶ Put the cracked ice cubes into a cocktail shaker. Pour the vodka, Strega, and orange juice over the ice. Shake vigorously until a frost forms.
❷ Strain into a chilled cocktail glass.

Variations

Golden Frog: put 4–6 crushed ice cubes into a blender or food processor and add 1 measure vodka, 1 measure Strega, 1 measure Galliano, and 1 measure lemon juice. Blend until slushy. Pour into a chilled cocktail glass.

Genoese: put 4–6 cracked ice cubes into a cocktail shaker. Pour 1 measure vodka, 1 measure grappa, ½ measure Sambuca, and ½ measure dry vermouth over the ice. Shake vigorously until a frost forms, then strain into a chilled cocktail glass.

White Spider: put 4–6 cracked ice cubes into a mixing glass. Pour 1 measure vodka and 1 measure white crème de menthe over the ice. Stir well to mix, then strain into a chilled cocktail glass.

Tailgate: put 4–6 cracked ice cubes into a mixing glass. Dash orange bitters over the ice and pour in 2 measures vodka, 1 measure green Chartreuse, and 1 measure sweet vermouth. Stir well, then strain into a chilled cocktail glass.

Full Monty

The expression "full monty," meaning not holding anything back, has been around for a long time, but was given a new lease of life by the highly successful British movie of the same title. However, you can keep your clothes on when mixing and drinking this cocktail.

serves 1

4–6 cracked ice cubes
1 measure vodka
1 measure Galliano
grated ginseng root, to decorate

❶ Put the cracked ice cubes into a cocktail shaker. Pour the vodka and Galliano over the ice. Shake vigorously until a frost forms.

❷ Strain into a chilled cocktail glass and sprinkle with grated ginseng root.

Cinematic cocktails

Back to the Future: put 4–6 cracked ice cubes into a cocktail shaker. Pour 2 measures gin, 1 measure slivovitz, and 1 measure lemon juice over the ice. Shake vigorously until a frost forms. Strain into a chilled cocktail glass.

Star Wars: put 4–6 cracked ice cubes into a cocktail shaker. Pour 2 measures gin, 2 measures lemon juice, 1 measure Galliano, and 1 measure crème de noyaux over the ice. Shake vigorously until a frost forms. Strain into a chilled cocktail glass.

Titanic: put 4–6 cracked ice cubes into a cocktail shaker. Pour 3 measures Mandarine Napoléon and 2 measures vodka over the ice. Shake vigorously until a frost forms. Half-fill a chilled glass with cracked ice cubes and strain the cocktail over them. Top off with sparkling mineral water.

Last Mango in Paris: put 4–6 cracked ice cubes into a blender or food processor and add 2 measures vodka, 1 measure crème de framboise, 1 measure lime juice, 2 halved strawberries, and ½ peeled and chopped fresh mango. Blend until slushy. Pour into a chilled goblet. Decorate with a lime slice and a strawberry.

What the Hell

Cheer yourself up when you are at a loose end, or when everything seems to have gone wrong, with this simple but delicious concoction.

serves 1

4–6 cracked ice cubes
dash of lime juice
1 measure gin
1 measure apricot brandy
1 measure dry vermouth
lemon peel twist, to decorate

❶ Put the cracked ice cubes into a mixing glass. Dash the lime juice over the ice and pour in the gin, apricot brandy, and vermouth. Stir well to mix.

❷ Strain into a chilled glass and decorate with the lemon peel twist.

Silly questions and answers

Why Not: put 4–6 cracked ice cubes into a mixing glass. Dash lemon juice over the ice and pour in 2 measures gin, 1 measure peach brandy, and 1 measure Noilly Prat. Stir to mix. Strain into a chilled glass.

Is This All: put 4–6 cracked ice cubes into a cocktail shaker. Pour 2 measures lemon vodka, 1 measure triple sec, and 1 measure lemon juice over the ice, and add 1 egg white. Shake until a frost forms, then strain into a chilled cocktail glass.

What The Dickens: pour 2 measures gin into a heatproof glass and stir in 1½ teaspoons confectioners' sugar. Top off with hot water.

This Is It: put 4–6 cracked ice cubes into a cocktail shaker. Pour 2 measures gin, 1 measure triple sec, and 1 measure lemon juice over the ice, and then add 1 egg white. Shake vigorously until a frost forms, then strain the mixture into a chilled cocktail glass.

Did you know?

French vermouth, of which Noilly Prat is the leading brand, is almost always dry, whereas sweet red vermouth is still the most popular type in Italy, although all the well-known brands—Martini, Cinzano, and Gancia—also include a dry version. Each firm keeps its own formula secret.

Nonalcoholic Cocktails

Lip Smacker

So many delicious ingredients are now available that nonalcoholic cocktails have come into their own. This one has all the kick of an alcoholic cocktail.

serves 1

4–6 crushed ice cubes

1 small tomato, peeled, seeded, and chopped

1 measure orange juice

2 tsp lime juice

1 scallion, chopped

1 small fresh red chile, seeded and chopped

pinch of superfine sugar

pinch of salt

dash of Tabasco sauce

To decorate

slice of lime and a chile rosette (see right)

❶ Put the crushed ice, tomato, orange juice, lime juice, scallion, and chile into a blender or food processor and process until smooth.

❷ Pour into a chilled glass, and stir in sugar, salt, and Tabasco sauce. Decorate with a lime slice and a chile rosette. To make a rosette, use a sharp knife to make 5 or 6 cuts ½ inch/1 cm from the stem end to the tip of a long, thin chile. Place in iced water for 30 minutes, until fanned out.

Variations

Hot Lips: substitute the flesh of ¼ small avocado for the tomato and a deseeded and chopped green chile for the red chile. **Open Prairie Oyster**: dash Tabasco sauce and white wine vinegar into a wine glass and pour in 1 teaspoon Worcestershire sauce and 1 measure tomato juice. Stir and add 1 egg yolk. Drink down in one, without breaking the egg yolk.

Did you know?

Sun-ripened tomatoes have a much sweeter and more concentrated flavor than those grown under glass or in polytunnels. Home-grown varieties are best, but those sold on the vine are a good buy.

Little Prince

Sparkling apple juice is a useful ingredient in nonalcoholic cocktails because it adds flavor and color, as well as fizz. Try using it as a substitute for champagne in nonalcoholic versions of cocktails such as Buck's Fizz (see page 66).

serves 1

4–6 cracked ice cubes
1 measure apricot juice
1 measure lemon juice
2 measures sparkling apple juice
lemon peel twist, to decorate

❶ Put the cracked ice cubes into a mixing glass. Pour the apricot juice, lemon juice, and apple juice over the ice and stir well.
❷ Strain into a chilled highball glass and decorate with the lemon peel twist.

An apple a day

Apple Frazzle: put 4–6 cracked ice cubes into a cocktail shaker. Pour 4 measures apple juice, 1 teaspoon sugar syrup (see page 11), and ½ teaspoon lemon juice over the ice. Shake vigorously until a frost forms. Strain into a chilled glass and top off with sparkling mineral water.

Bite of the Apple: put 4–6 crushed ice cubes into a blender or food processor and add 5 measures apple juice, 1 measure lime juice, ½ teaspoon orgeat, and 1 tablespoon apple sauce or apple purée. Blend until smooth. Pour into a chilled glass. Sprinkle with ground cinnamon.

Prohibition Punch (to serve 25): pour 3¾ cups apple juice, 1½ cups lemon juice, and ½ cup sugar syrup (see page 11) into a large pitcher. Add cracked ice cubes and 9 cups ginger ale. Stir gently to mix. Serve in chilled glasses, decorated with slices of orange and with straws.

Red Apple Sunset: put 4–6 cracked ice cubes into a cocktail shaker. Dash grenadine over the ice and pour in 2 measures apple juice and 2 measures grapefruit juice. Shake vigorously until a frost forms. Strain into a chilled cocktail glass.

Grapefruit Cooler

This is a wonderfully refreshing drink that is ideal for serving at a family barbecue. Start making this at least two hours before you want to serve it, to have plenty of time for the mint to steep in the syrup.

serves 6

2 well-packed cups fresh mint leaves

2 measures sugar syrup (see page 11)

2 cups grapefruit juice

4 measures lemon juice

about 30 cracked ice cubes

sparkling mineral water, to top off

fresh mint sprigs, to decorate

❶ Crush the fresh mint leaves and place in a small bowl. Add the sugar syrup and stir well. Let stand for at least 2 hours to soak, mashing the mint with a spoon from time to time.

❷ Strain the syrup into a pitcher and add the grapefruit juice and lemon juice. Cover with plastic wrap and chill in the refrigerator for at least 2 hours.

❸ To serve, fill 6 chilled Collins glasses with cracked ice cubes. Divide the cocktail among the glasses and top off with sparkling mineral water. Decorate with fresh mint sprigs.

Cool it

Bright Green Cooler (serves 1): put 4–6 cracked ice cubes into a cocktail shaker. Pour 3 measures pineapple juice, 2 measures lime juice, and 1 measure green peppermint syrup over the ice. Shake the mixture vigorously until a frost forms. Half-fill a tall, chilled tumbler with cracked ice cubes and then strain the cocktail over them. Top up with ginger ale and decorate with a slice of cucumber and a lime slice.

Did you know?

There is a green-skinned grapefruit variety called "Sweetie" that is less sharp than the yellow-skinned fruits. Pink grapefruit is also slightly milder in flavor.

Shirley Temple

This is one of the most famous of classic nonalcoholic cocktails. Shirley Temple Black became a respected diplomat, but this cocktail dates from the days when she was an immensely popular child movie star in the 1930s.

serves 1

8–10 cracked ice cubes
2 measures lemon juice
1/2 measure grenadine
1/2 measure sugar syrup (see page 11)
ginger ale, to top off

To decorate
orange slice
maraschino cherry

❶ Put 4–6 cracked ice cubes into a cocktail shaker. Pour the lemon juice, grenadine, and sugar syrup over the ice and shake vigorously.

❷ Half-fill a small, chilled glass with cracked ice cubes and strain the cocktail over them. Top off with ginger ale. Decorate with the orange slice and maraschino cherry.

Other classics

St. Clements: put 6–8 cracked ice cubes into a chilled glass. Pour 2 measures orange juice and 2 measures bitter lemon over the ice. Stir gently and decorate with orange and lemon slices.

Black and Tan: pour 2/3 cup chilled ginger ale into a chilled glass. Add 2/3 cup chilled ginger beer. Do not stir. Decorate with a lime wedge.

Tea Punch: put 4–6 cracked ice cubes into a mixing glass. Pour 3 measures cold black tea, 3 measures orange juice, 3 measures sparkling apple juice, and 1 1/2 measures lemon juice over the ice. Stir well to mix, then pour into a tall, chilled glass. Decorate with a lemon slice.

Beachcomber: put 4–6 cracked ice cubes into a cocktail shaker. Pour 2/3 cup guava juice, 2 measures lime juice, and 1 measure raspberry syrup over the ice. Shake vigorously until a frost forms, then pour into a chilled glass.

Melon Medley

Choose a very ripe, sweet-fleshed melon, such as a cantaloupe, for this lovely, fresh-tasting cocktail. This drink is perfect for sipping on a hot evening.

serves 1

4–6 crushed ice cubes

½ cup diced melon flesh

4 measures orange juice

½ measure lemon juice

❶ Put the crushed ice into a blender or food processor and add the diced melon. Pour in the orange juice and lemon juice. Blend until slushy.

❷ Pour into a chilled Collins glass.

Sweet and juicy

River Cruise (to serve 6): put 8 cups diced cantaloupe melon flesh into a blender or food processor and process to a smooth purée. Scrape into a pitcher. Put the grated rind and juice of 2 lemons and 2 tablespoons sugar into a small pan. Heat gently, stirring until the sugar has dissolved. Pour the lemon syrup over the melon purée and let cool. Then cover with plastic wrap and chill in the refrigerator for at least 2 hours. To serve, half-fill 6 chilled glasses with cracked ice. Stir the melon mixture and divide it among the glasses. Top off with sparkling mineral water and decorate with melon wedges and cocktail cherries.

Kool Kevin: put 4–6 crushed ice cubes into a blender or food processor and add ½ cup diced cantaloupe melon flesh, 1 measure grenadine, and 1 measure heavy cream. Blend until smooth. Pour into a small, chilled glass. Add 1 measure ginger ale and stir gently. Sprinkle with ground ginger and decorate with a melon wedge.

Smoothies

& Juices

It is no surprise that smoothies and mixed juices have become so fashionable in these health-conscious days. Commercial soft drinks and even some fruit juices often contain ingredients that many of us would rather avoid—artificial colorings and flavorings, high levels of sugar or chemical sweeteners, and preservatives. In addition, many of them are so sickly, bland,

or unexciting that they simply do not appeal to the adult palate. Making fruit and vegetable drinks at home ensures that we know precisely what they contain. It also means that we can mix them to taste truly delicious. What is more, we can guarantee that the raw ingredients are organic, if that's what we want.

Nutritionists recommend that we should eat at least five portions of fruit and vegetables a day. Modern life is so busy, however, that few of us have the time or inclination to plan, shop, prepare, and cook balanced meals every day of the week. The good news is that in the few minutes it takes to juice a handful of carrots and tomatoes, or to whizz some berries and yogurt in the food

processor, we can produce the equivalent of one of those portions. Better still, the ingredients are usually raw and the juice or smoothie will be consumed immediately. So there is less possibility of nutrients leaching out during cooking or being destroyed through excessive exposure to air. This makes the drink even healthier.

You can make smoothies and juices from most fruit and vegetables. The golden rule is never to combine the two, with the exceptions of apples and carrots, which go with just about everything, and tomatoes, a fruit that most treat as a vegetable. The following recipes will give you an excellent starting point, and should provide you with lots of ideas for inventing your own drinks. Generally, once people have begun the habit of making their own fruit and vegetable drinks, they become great enthusiasts and never feel the need to return to commercial brands.

Of course, smoothies and juices are enjoyable thirst quenchers, but there is much more to them than this. Many provide a powerful boost that can kick-start the day at breakfast time or revive flagging energy in the afternoon, with a healthy nutritional balance that you won't find in a packet of cookies or a chocolate bar. Bananas, for example, are full of natural sugar, which provides a source of rapidly released energy. Citrus fruits, berries, and, above all, kiwifruit are packed with vitamin C; strawberries

and raspberries contain iron; and carrots are a valuable source of betacarotene. In addition, with a juicer (see page 102), some of the fiber is incorporated in the drink and not discarded.

The following recipes are divided into three sections—Fruits, Vegetables, Herbs & Spices, and Sweets & Coffees. The selection of delicious drinks not only includes smoothies and mixed juices, but also coolers and other long drinks; pick-me-ups; tea- and coffee-based mixes; and some lovely milkshakes for a special treat. You will also find some useful information about equipment and ways of preparing ingredients to set you on the right path to complete success in making your own healthy and tasty fruit and vegetable concoctions.

Equipment

Making smoothies and juices is great fun, as well as being very healthy. All you need are the right ingredients and equipment, some recipes, and your imagination. You don't have to spend a lot of money on equipment, but for the best and freshest results, you will need a food processor and a juicer.

A basic kitchen food processor with a standard metal blade mixes smoothies to perfection in a few moments, and the following recipes assume that one will be used. You might also be able to use a blender, depending on how robust the model is. However, unless your food processor has a juicer attachment, you cannot use it for making juice, because it will just turn

the ingredients into a purée. A juicer, on the other hand, separates the pulp from the juice. There are three types of juicer, and these vary considerably in price. Centrifugal juicers are at the lower end of the price range. Coarsely chopped ingredients are fed into this type of machine, which grates them into tiny pieces and spins them at high speed. The liquid is extracted by centrifugal force, leaving the fruit or vegetable pulp behind. As the fruit and vegetables are exposed to the air throughout the process, juices made by this method are thought to have the lowest nutritional content.

Hydraulic juicers are at the top end of the price range. Extreme pressure forces the juice out of the ingredients, through a strainer and into a pitcher, leaving the pulp behind. Juices pressed by this method are very high in nutrients.

The third type, triturating juicers, are in the middle of the price range and the juice they produce is in the middle of the nutritional range. A rotating cutter tears up the ingredients and simultaneously presses them against a strainer.

Besides cost, other aspects to consider before buying a juicer are size—triturating juicers tend to be larger than the others—the speed at which they work, and how easy they are to clean. But whichever type of juicer you choose, you can still be sure that the drink you are creating will be full of nutrients as well as flavor.

Any other equipment you are likely to need, from a cutting board to an ice-cube tray, you will almost certainly already have in your kitchen cupboards. You should never use a cutting board used for meat for preparing fruit and vegetables.

Techniques

When you use a food processor, everything that goes into the goblet will be incorporated into the final drink. Consequently, fruit and vegetables must be washed, peeled, and prepared in the same way as for any other type of recipe. Pits, pips, and seeds must all be removed. Large, firm fruit and vegetables, such as apples and carrots, should be roughly chopped before being placed in the processor.

If you are going to add ice cubes to the food processor, they need to be crushed before they are added.. See page 11 for instructions on how to crush ice cubes.

The technique with juicers, whatever type you are using, is different because the juice and solid residue are kept separate. Most vegetables and fruits, with the obvious exceptions of bananas, kiwifruit, and citrus fruits, do not need to be peeled. However, it is still important that they are thoroughly washed.

Some juicers can cope with quite tough skins, even including the skins of melons. Many of the nutrients in fruits lie just below the surface of the skin, so this is a particularly valuable asset, but it does mean that you must be sure to use specimens with undamaged skin.

As a rough guide to making your own fresh juices, 1 lb 2 oz/500 g of carrots or apples yields a scant 1 cup/225 ml of juice while 1 lb 2 oz/500 g of tomatoes or blackberries will produce a generous 1½ cups/325 ml of fresh juice.

You can leave vegetable tops, such as beet leaves, attached, but do trim off the roots. Coarse outer leaves that would be removed for other culinary purposes don't need trimming. Pits, such as those in cherries, peaches, and mangoes, should be removed, but you can leave smaller seeds and pips in grapes, apples, and pears. Then the process of actually making the juice is very simple.

Fruits

Melon Smoothie

**This summer smoothie, with three different kinds of melon,
is deliciously refreshing on a hot day.**

serves 2

1 cup plain yogurt

¾ cup peeled, seeded, and coarsely
chopped honeydew melon

¾ cup peeled, seeded, and coarsely
chopped cantaloupe melon

¾ cup peeled, seeded, and coarsely
chopped watermelon

6 ice cubes

wedges of melon, to decorate

Method

❶ Pour the yogurt into a food processor. Add the honeydew melon pieces and process until smooth.

❷ Add the cantaloupe and watermelon pieces along with the ice cubes and process until smooth. Pour the mixture into 2 glasses and decorate with wedges of melon. Serve immediately.

Nectarine Melt

Mango and nectarine is an inspired combination, made all the more special with the clever addition of lemon sherbet.

serves 2

1 cup milk

2 cups lemon sherbet

1 ripe mango, peeled, pitted, and diced

2 ripe nectarines, peeled, pitted, and diced

Method

❶ Pour the milk into a food processor, add half the lemon sherbet, and process gently until combined. Add the remaining sherbet and process until smooth.

❷ When the mixture is thoroughly blended, gradually add the mango and nectarines and process until smooth. Pour the mixture into 2 glasses and add straws and serve.

Orange & Lime Iced Tea

Sweet and sharp citrus flavors turn a very simple drink into a subtle and sophisticated thirst-quencher.

serves 2

1¼ cups water	**To decorate**
2 tea bags	lime wedge
scant ½ cup orange juice	sugar
4 tbsp lime juice	orange, lemon, or lime slices
1–2 tbsp brown sugar	
8 ice cubes	

Method

❶ Pour the water into a pan and bring to a boil. Remove the pan from the heat, then add the tea bags and let infuse for 5 minutes. Remove the tea bags and let the tea cool for 30 minutes, or until room temperature. Transfer to a pitcher, then cover with plastic wrap and chill in the refrigerator for at least 45 minutes.

❷ When the tea has chilled, pour in the orange juice and lime juice. Add brown sugar to taste.

❸ Take 2 glasses and rub the rims with a lime wedge, then dip them in sugar to frost. Put the ice cubes into the glasses and pour over the tea. Decorate the rims with orange, lemon, or lime slices and serve immediately.

Fruit Cooler

Power up with breakfast in a glass, packed with protein, vitamins, and slow-release carbohydrate—and a sensational flavor, too.

serves 2

1 cup orange juice

½ cup plain yogurt

2 eggs

2 bananas, peeled, sliced, and frozen

fresh banana slices, to decorate

Method

❶ Pour the orange juice and yogurt into a food processor and process gently until combined.

❷ Add the eggs and frozen banana slices and process until smooth. Pour the mixture into 2 glasses and decorate the rims with fresh banana slices. Add straws and serve immediately.

Spicy Banana Chill

A Caribbean combo to tantalize the taste buds with just a hint of heat in every mouthful of icy sweetness.

serves 2

1¼ cups milk

½ tsp mixed spice

¾ cup banana ice cream

2 bananas, peeled, sliced, and frozen

Method

❶ Pour the milk into a food processor and add the mixed spice. Add half the banana ice cream and process gently until combined, then add the remaining ice cream and process until well blended.

❷ When the mixture is well combined, add the frozen banana slices and process until smooth. Pour the mixture into 2 tall glasses and add straws. Serve immediately.

Cranberry Energizer

Top up your vitamin C levels—this is the perfect pick-me-up for getting going and waking up a sluggish system.

serves 2

1¼ cups cranberry juice

scant ½ cup orange juice

1 cup fresh raspberries

1 tbsp lemon juice

lemon or orange slices and spirals, to decorate

Method

❶ Pour the cranberry juice and orange juice into a food processor and process gently until combined. Add the raspberries and lemon juice and process until smooth.

❷ Pour the mixture into 2 glasses and decorate with the lemon or orange slices and spirals speared on toothpicks. Serve immediately.

Caribbean Cocktail

Chill out with a tropical treat. If you close your eyes, you can almost hear
the waves lapping on the beach.

serves 2

scant ½ cup coconut milk

scant 1 cup soy milk

scant ½ cup pineapple juice

1 tbsp brown sugar

1 ripe mango, peeled, pitted, and diced

2 tbsp grated fresh coconut

1 cup frozen pineapple chunks

1 banana, peeled, sliced, and frozen

To decorate

grated fresh coconut

fresh pineapple wedges

Method

❶ Put the coconut milk, soy milk,
pineapple juice, and sugar into a food
processor and process gently until
combined. Add the diced mango to the
food processor along with the grated
coconut and process well.

❷ Add the frozen pineapple chunks and
banana slices and process until smooth.
Pour the mixture into 2 glasses, then
sprinkle over some grated coconut and
decorate the rims with fresh pineapple
wedges. Serve immediately.

Pineapple Soda

Ice cream soda for grown-ups, this luscious mix of pineapple, coconut milk, and vanilla ice cream is irresistible.

serves 2

¾ cup pineapple juice

scant ½ cup coconut milk

1 cup vanilla ice cream

1 cup frozen pineapple chunks

¾ cup sparkling water

2 scooped-out pineapple shells (optional)

Method

❶ Pour the pineapple juice and coconut milk into a food processor. Add the ice cream and process until smooth.

❷ Add the frozen pineapple chunks and process well. Pour the mixture into 2 scooped-out pineapple shells or tall glasses until two-thirds full. Top up with sparkling water, add straws, and serve.

Pineapple & Coconut Shake

**The perfect partnership—and a lovely way to wind down at the end of a busy day
with your own perfect partner.**

serves 2

1½ cups pineapple juice

scant ½ cup coconut milk

¾ cup vanilla ice cream

1 cup frozen pineapple chunks

2 scooped-out coconut shells (optional)

2 tbsp grated fresh coconut, to decorate

Method

❶ Pour the pineapple juice and coconut milk into a food processor. Add the ice cream and process until smooth.

❷ Add the frozen pineapple chunks and process until smooth. Pour the mixture into 2 scooped-out coconut shells or tall glasses, and decorate with grated fresh coconut. Add straws and serve.

Peach & Pineapple Smoothie

Sweet and creamy with a hint of sharpness, this elegant smoothie will appeal to sophisticated palates.

serves 2

½ cup pineapple juice

juice of 1 lemon

scant ½ cup water

3 tbsp brown sugar

¾ cup plain yogurt

1 ripe peach, peeled, pitted, cut into chunks, and frozen

¾ cup frozen pineapple chunks

fresh pineapple wedges, to decorate

Method

❶ Pour the pineapple juice, lemon juice, and water into a food processor. Add the sugar and yogurt and process until blended.

❷ Add the frozen peach and pineapple chunks and process until smooth. Pour the mixture into glasses and decorate the rims with fresh pineapple wedges. Serve immediately.

Pineapple Crush

A long, cool thirst-quencher, this will boost your concentration
and revitalize a tired or stressed mind.

serves 2

scant ½ cup pineapple juice

4 tbsp orange juice

¾ cup peeled, seeded, and coarsely
chopped melon

1 cup frozen pineapple chunks

4 ice cubes

To decorate

fresh melon slices

fresh orange slices

Method

❶ Pour the pineapple juice and orange
juice into a food processor and process
gently until combined.

❷ Add the melon, frozen pineapple,
and ice cubes and process until a slushy
consistency has been reached.

❸ Pour the mixture into 2 glasses and
decorate with fresh melon and orange
slices. Serve immediately.

Hawaiian Shake

When your energy levels are flagging, give yourself a treat with this invigorating
and exuberant shake.

serves 2

1 cup milk

3½ tbsp coconut milk

¾ cup vanilla ice cream

2 bananas, peeled, sliced, and frozen

1 cup canned pineapple chunks, drained

1 papaya, seeded and diced

To decorate

grated fresh coconut

fresh pineapple wedges

Method

❶ Pour the milk and coconut milk into a food processor and process gently until combined. Add half the ice cream and process gently, then add the remaining ice cream and process until smooth.

❷ Add the frozen banana slices and process well, then add the pineapple chunks and papaya and process until smooth. Pour the mixture into 2 tall glasses, then sprinkle over the grated coconut and decorate the rims with pineapple wedges. Serve immediately.

Pacific Smoothie

Luscious figs combine superbly with the nuts, orange juice, and maple syrup in this unusual and delicate drink.

serves 2

1½ cups hazelnut yogurt

2 tbsp freshly squeezed orange juice

4 tbsp maple syrup

8 large fresh figs, peeled and chopped

6 ice cubes

toasted chopped hazelnuts, to decorate

Method

❶ Pour the yogurt, orange juice, and maple syrup into a food processor and process gently until combined.

❷ Add the figs and ice cubes and process until smooth. Pour the mixture into 2 glasses and sprinkle over some toasted chopped hazelnuts. Serve immediately.

Rose Sunset

This beautifully fragrant drink, with its romantic name, has an equally delectable and illusive flavor.

serves 2

scant ½ cup plain yogurt

2 cups milk

1 tbsp rose water

3 tbsp honey

1 ripe mango, pitted, peeled, and diced

6 ice cubes

edible rose petals, to decorate (optional)

Method

❶ Pour the yogurt and milk into a food processor and process gently until combined.

❷ Add the rose water and honey and process until thoroughly blended, then add the mango along with the ice cubes and process until smooth. Pour the mixture into 2 glasses, then decorate with edible rose petals, if using, and serve.

Fruit Rapture

Simple, but splendid, this restorative smoothie will get you back on track at any time of day.

serves 2

scant ½ cup milk

½ cup peach yogurt

scant ½ cup orange juice

8 oz/225 g canned peach slices, drained

6 ice cubes

fresh orange peel strips, to decorate

Method

❶ Pour the milk, yogurt, and orange juice into a food processor and process gently until combined.

❷ Add the peach slices and ice cubes and process until smooth. Pour the mixture into 2 glasses and decorate with fresh orange peel strips. Add straws and serve.

Traditional Lemonade

This classic cooler, redolent of a more leisured and peaceful era,
is a well-loved favorite.

serves 2

⅔ cup water

6 tbsp sugar

1 tsp grated lemon rind

½ cup lemon juice

6 ice cubes

sparkling water

To decorate

lemon wedge

sugar

lemon slices

Method

❶ Put the water, sugar, and grated lemon rind into a small pan and bring to a boil, stirring constantly. Continue to boil, stirring, for 5 minutes.

❷ Remove the pan from the heat and let cool for 30 minutes, or until room temperature. Stir in the lemon juice, then transfer to a pitcher and cover with plastic wrap. Let chill for at least 2 hours.

❸ When the lemon mixture has almost finished chilling, take 2 glasses and rub the rims with a lemon wedge, then dip them in sugar to frost. Put the ice cubes into the glasses.

❹ Remove the lemon mixture from the refrigerator, then pour it over the ice and top up with sparkling water. The ratio should be 1 part lemon mixture to 3 parts sparkling water. Stir well to mix, then decorate with fresh lemon slices and serve immediately.

Kiwi Dream

More than a whole day's dose of vitamin C in a glass, as well as a wonderfully refreshing sweet and sharp flavor.

serves 2

⅔ cup milk

juice of 2 limes

2 kiwifruit, peeled and chopped

1 tbsp sugar

2 cups vanilla ice cream

To decorate

kiwifruit slices

lime peel strips

Method

❶ Pour the milk and lime juice into a food processor and process gently until combined.

❷ Add the kiwifruit and sugar and process gently, then add the ice cream and process until smooth. Pour the mixture into 2 glasses and decorate with kiwifruit slices and lime peel strips. Serve immediately.

Banana & Apple Booster

Kick-start your day and wake up your taste buds with this zingy vitamin- and mineral-packed energizer.

serves 2

1 cup apple juice

½ tsp ground cinnamon

2 tsp grated fresh gingerroot

2 bananas, peeled, sliced, and frozen

fresh banana slices, to decorate

Method

❶ Pour the apple juice into a food processor. Add the cinnamon and gingerroot and process gently until combined.

❷ Add the frozen banana slices and process until smooth. Pour the mixture into 2 tall glasses and decorate with fresh banana slices speared on toothpicks. Serve immediately.

Banana & Blueberry Smoothie

Sweet, sharp, fragrant, rich, and creamy, this is pure magic-in-a-glass that will lift your spirits.

serves 2

¾ cup apple juice

½ cup plain yogurt

1 banana, peeled, sliced, and frozen

1 cup frozen blueberries

whole fresh blueberries, to decorate

Method

❶ Pour the apple juice into a food processor. Add the yogurt and process until smooth.

❷ Add the frozen banana slices and half the frozen blueberries and process well, then add the remaining blueberries and process until smooth. Pour the mixture into 2 tall glasses and decorate with whole fresh blueberries. Add straws and serve.

Raspberry Cooler

Liquid sunshine—not only is this superbly refreshing, but it also tones the whole system.

serves 2

8 crushed ice cubes

2 tbsp raspberry syrup

2 cups chilled apple juice

whole fresh raspberries and

apple pieces, to decorate

Method

❶ Divide the crushed ice between 2 glasses. Pour the raspberry syrup over the ice.

❷ Top up each glass with chilled apple juice and stir well. Decorate with the whole fresh raspberries and apple pieces speared on toothpicks and serve immediately.

Berry Cream

The inspired combination of sweet banana and tart summer berries could almost be described as intoxicating.

serves 2

1½ cups orange juice

1 lb/450 g frozen berries
(such as blueberries, raspberries,
and blackberries)

1 banana, peeled, sliced, and frozen

fresh strawberry slices, to decorate

Method

❶ Pour the orange juice into a food processor. Add half the frozen berries and the banana slices and process until smooth.

❷ Add the remaining berries and process until smooth. Pour the mixture into 2 tall glasses and decorate the rims with strawberry slices. Add straws and serve immediately.

Strawberry & Orange Smoothie

Probably one of the first smoothies ever invented, this impeccable combination remains a firm favorite.

serves 2

½ cup plain yogurt

¾ cup strawberry yogurt

¾ cup orange juice

generous ½ cup frozen sliced strawberries

1 banana, peeled, sliced, and frozen

To decorate

orange slices

whole fresh strawberries

Method

❶ Pour the plain and strawberry yogurts into a food processor and process gently. Add the orange juice and process until the mixture is combined.

❷ Add the frozen strawberries and banana slices and process until smooth. Pour the mixture into 2 tall glasses and decorate with orange slices and whole fresh strawberries. Add straws and serve immediately.

Strawberry & Peach Smoothie

One luscious glassful of this wonderfully fruity mix and you will feel restored, revived, and refreshed.

serves 2

¾ cup milk

8 oz/225 g canned peach slices, drained

2 ripe apricots, peeled, pitted, and chopped

12–14 fresh strawberries, hulled and sliced

2 bananas, peeled, sliced, and frozen

fresh strawberry slices, to decorate

Method

❶ Pour the milk into a food processor. Add the peach slices and process gently until combined. Add the apricots and process gently until combined.

❷ Add the strawberries and banana slices and process until smooth. Pour the mixture into 2 glasses and decorate the rims with fresh strawberry slices. Add straws and serve immediately.

Summer & Citrus Fruit Punch

Serve this vibrant punch whenever you have something to celebrate, or just to make yourself feel good.

serves 2

4 tbsp orange juice

1 tbsp lime juice

scant ½ cup sparkling water

2 cups frozen summer fruits
(such as blueberries, raspberries,
blackberries, and strawberries)

4 ice cubes

whole fresh raspberries, black currants or
blueberries, and blackberries, to decorate

Method

❶ Pour the orange juice, lime juice, and sparkling water into a food processor. Process gently until combined.

❷ Add the frozen summer fruits and ice cubes and process until a slushy consistency has been reached.

❸ Pour the mixture into 2 glasses and decorate with fresh raspberries, black currants or blueberries, and blackberries speared on toothpicks, and serve immediately.

Cherry Kiss

This long and lively cooler is a welcome way to turn off the heat in the height of summer.

serves 2

8 ice cubes, crushed

2 tbsp cherry syrup

2 cups sparkling water

maraschino cherries, to decorate

Method

❶ Divide the crushed ice between 2 glasses and pour over the cherry syrup.

❷ Top up each glass with sparkling water. Decorate with the maraschino cherries speared on toothpicks and serve.

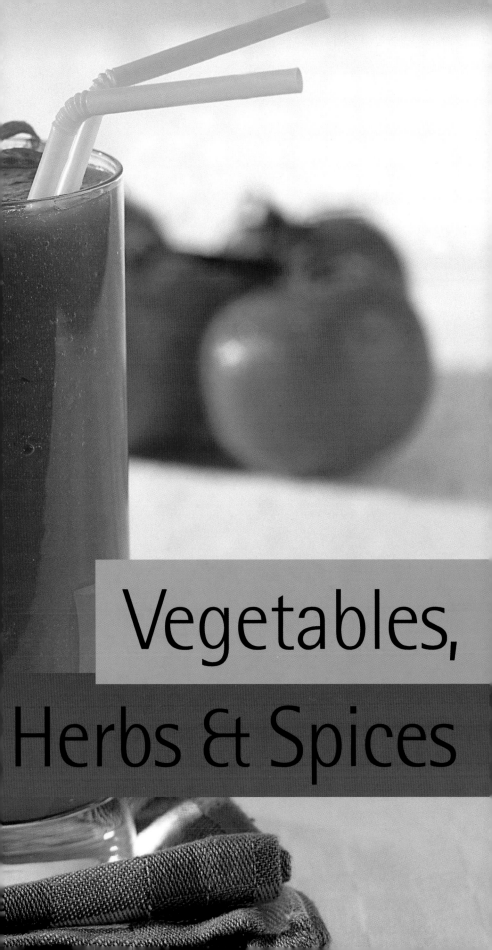

Vegetables, Herbs & Spices

Red Pepper Reactor

Boost your energy levels and fire up your system with this truly dynamic vegetable medley.

serves 2

1 cup carrot juice

1 cup tomato juice

2 large red bell peppers,
seeded and coarsely chopped

1 tbsp lemon juice

pepper, to serve

Method

1 Pour the carrot juice and tomato juice into a food processor and process gently until combined.

2 Add the bell peppers and lemon juice. Season with plenty of pepper and process until smooth. Pour the mixture into 2 tall glasses, add straws and serve immediately.

Ginger Crush

The sweet, mild flavors of carrot and tomato are literally gingered up in this enlivening drink.

serves 2

1 cup carrot juice

4 tomatoes, peeled, seeded, and coarsely chopped

1 tbsp lemon juice

½ cup coarsely chopped fresh parsley

1 tbsp grated fresh gingerroot

6 ice cubes

½ cup water

chopped fresh parsley, to garnish

Method

❶ Put the carrot juice, tomatoes, and lemon juice into a food processor and process gently until combined.

❷ Add the parsley to the food processor along with the ginger and ice cubes.

Process until well combined, then pour in the water and process until smooth.

❸ Pour the mixture into 2 tall glasses and garnish with chopped fresh parsley. Serve immediately.

Peppermint Ice

Simultaneously hot and cold on the tongue, this classic combination
still manages to surprise.

serves 2

⅔ cup milk

2 tbsp peppermint syrup

2 cups mint ice cream

fresh mint sprigs, to decorate

Method

❶ Pour the milk and peppermint syrup
into a food processor and process gently
until combined.

❷ Add the mint ice cream and process
until smooth. Pour the mixture into 2 tall
glasses and decorate with mint sprigs. Add
straws and serve.

Cinnamon & Lemon Tea

Enjoy this aromatic winter warmer and, at the same time, keep the worst of the weather and colds at bay.

serves 2

1¾ cups water

4 cloves

1 small cinnamon stick

2 tea bags

3–4 tbsp lemon juice

1–2 tbsp brown sugar

fresh lemon slices, to decorate

Method

❶ Put the water, cloves, and cinnamon into a pan and bring to a boil. Remove the pan from the heat and add the tea bags. Let infuse for 5 minutes, then remove the tea bags.

❷ Stir in lemon juice and sugar to taste. Return the pan to low heat and warm through gently. Do not boil.

❸ Remove the pan from the heat and strain the tea into 2 heatproof glasses. Decorate with fresh lemon slices and serve.

Celery Surprise

A savory delight that not only acts as a tonic, but also cleanses and refreshes the palate.

serves 2

½ cup carrot juice

1 lb/450 g tomatoes, peeled, seeded, and coarsely chopped

1 tbsp lemon juice

4 celery stalks, trimmed and sliced

4 scallions, roughly chopped

½ cup coarsely chopped fresh parsley

1 well-packed cup fresh mint leaves

2 celery stalks, to garnish

Method

❶ Put the carrot juice, tomatoes, and lemon juice into a food processor and process gently until combined.

❷ Add the sliced celery along with the scallions, parsley, and mint and process until smooth. Pour the mixture into 2 tall glasses and garnish with celery stalks. Serve immediately.

Curried Crush

**Juice with attitude—this stimulating blend of flavors is guaranteed
to add spice to your life.**

serves 2

1 cup carrot juice	1 garlic clove, chopped
4 tomatoes, peeled, seeded, and coarsely chopped	½ cup coarsely chopped fresh parsley
1 tbsp lemon juice	1 tsp curry powder
2 celery stalks, trimmed and sliced	6 ice cubes
1 small romaine lettuce	½ cup water
	2 celery stalks, to garnish

Method

❶ Put the carrot juice, tomatoes, lemon juice, and sliced celery into a food processor and process until combined.

❷ Separate the lettuce leaves, then wash them and add them to the food processor along with the garlic, parsley, curry powder, and ice cubes. Process until well combined, then pour in the water and process until smooth.

❸ Pour the mixture into 2 tall glasses and garnish with celery stalks. Serve immediately.

Watercress Float

Peppery watercress perks up carrot juice and provides extra vitamins and minerals in this cleansing drink. If watercress is unavailable, use arugula instead.

serves 2

2 cups carrot juice

½ cup watercress or arugula leaves

1 tbsp lemon juice

watercress or arugula sprigs, to garnish

Method

❶ Pour the carrot juice into a food processor. Add the watercress and lemon juice and process until smooth. Transfer to a pitcher, then cover with plastic wrap and let chill in the refrigerator for at least 1 hour, or until required.

❷ When the mixture is thoroughly chilled, pour into 2 glasses and garnish with fresh watercress sprigs. Serve immediately.

Orange & Carrot Shake

This doesn't just taste and look fabulous, but contains abundant, health-giving betacarotene and vitamin C.

serves 2

¾ cup carrot juice

¾ cup orange juice

¾ cup vanilla ice cream

6 ice cubes

To decorate

orange slices

orange peel strips

Method

❶ Pour the carrot juice and orange juice into a food processor and process gently until well combined. Add the ice cream and process until thoroughly blended.

❷ Add the ice cubes and process until smooth. Pour the mixture into 2 glasses and decorate with orange slices and orange peel strips. Serve.

Red Storm

A surefire lip-smacker, this spicy little number is definitely not for the unwary or faint-hearted.

serves 2

2 cups tomato juice

dash of Worcestershire sauce

1 small fresh red chile, seeded and chopped

1 scallion, trimmed and chopped

6 ice cubes

2 long, thin red chiles, cut into flowers (see below), to garnish

Method

❶ To make the chile flowers for the garnish, use a small sharp knife to make 6 cuts along each chile. Place the tip of the knife about ½ inch/1 cm from the stem end and cut toward the tip. Put the chiles in a bowl of iced water and leave them for 25–30 minutes, or until they have spread out into flower shapes.

❷ Put the tomato juice and Worcestershire sauce into a food processor and process gently until combined. Add the chopped chile, scallion, and ice cubes and process until smooth.

❸ Pour the mixture into 2 glasses and garnish with the chile flowers. Add straws and serve immediately.

Sweets
& Coffees

Rich Chocolate Shake

**The ultimate milkshake for children and chocoholics of all ages,
this is supremely satisfying.**

serves 2

⅔ cup milk

2 tbsp chocolate syrup

2 cups chocolate ice cream

grated chocolate, to decorate

Method

❶ Pour the milk and chocolate syrup into a food processor and process gently until combined.

❷ Add the chocolate ice cream and process until smooth. Pour the mixture into 2 tall glasses and sprinkle the grated chocolate over the top. Serve immediately.

Maple & Almond Milkshake

Go on. Why not indulge your sweet tooth with this rather grown-up, rich-tasting, novel milkshake?

serves 2

⅔ cup milk

2 tbsp maple syrup

2 cups vanilla ice cream

1 tbsp almond extract

chopped almonds, to decorate

Method

❶ Pour the milk and maple syrup into a food processor and process gently until combined.

❷ Add the ice cream and almond extract and process until smooth. Pour the mixture into 2 tall glasses and decorate with chopped almonds and add straws. Serve.

Coffee Whip

The magical pairing of coffee and chocolate can be improved only by the addition of whipped cream.

serves 2

¾ cup milk

3½ tbsp light cream

1 tbsp brown sugar

2 tbsp unsweetened cocoa powder

1 tbsp coffee syrup or

instant coffee powder

6 ice cubes

To decorate

whipped cream

grated chocolate

Method

❶ Put the milk, cream, and sugar into a food processor and process gently until combined.

❷ Add the cocoa powder and coffee syrup or powder and process well, then add the ice cubes and process until smooth.

❸ Pour the mixture into 2 glasses. Top with whipped cream and sprinkle over the grated chocolate. Serve.

Banana & Coffee Milkshake

A powerhouse drink for those who lead life on the run, this unusual milkshake tastes great, too.

serves 2

1 ¼ cups milk

4 tbsp instant coffee powder

¾ cup vanilla ice cream

2 bananas, peeled, sliced, and frozen

Method

❶ Pour the milk into a food processor, then add the coffee powder and process gently until combined. Add half the vanilla ice cream and process gently, then add the remaining ice cream and process until well combined.

❷ When the mixture is thoroughly blended, add the frozen banana slices and process until smooth. Pour the mixture into 2 tall glasses and serve.

Smooth Iced Coffee

Nothing could be nicer after a long, lazy, alfresco lunch than this cool, elegant iced coffee.

serves 2

1¾ cups water

2 tbsp instant coffee crystals

2 tbsp brown sugar

6 ice cubes

To decorate

light cream

whole coffee beans

Method

❶ Use the water and coffee crystals to brew some hot coffee, then let cool for 30 minutes, or until room temperature. Transfer to a pitcher, then cover with plastic wrap and let chill in the refrigerator for at least 45 minutes.

❷ When the coffee has chilled, pour it into a food processor. Add the sugar and process until well combined. Add the ice cubes and process until smooth.

❸ Pour the mixture into 2 tall glasses. Float cream on the top and decorate with whole coffee beans. Serve.

Hazelnut & Coffee Sparkle

Try something a little different—you will be pleasantly surprised by how successful this mix is.

serves 2

1 cup water

3 tbsp instant coffee crystals

½ cup sparkling water

1 tbsp hazelnut syrup

2 tbsp brown sugar

6 ice cubes

To decorate

lime slices

lemon slices

Method

❶ Use the water and coffee crystals to brew some hot coffee, then let cool for 30 minutes, or until room temperature. Transfer to a pitcher, then cover with plastic wrap and let chill in the refrigerator for at least 45 minutes.

❷ When the coffee has chilled, pour it into a food processor. Add the sparkling water, hazelnut syrup, and sugar and process well. Add the ice cubes and process until smooth.

❸ Pour the mixture into 2 tall glasses and decorate the rims with lime and lemon slices. Serve.

Peppermint Mocha

**This exhilarating fusion of flavors could certainly set tongues wagging—
but only with sheer delight.**

serves 2

1¾ cups milk

¾ cup coffee syrup

scant ½ cup peppermint syrup

1 tbsp chopped fresh mint leaves

4 ice cubes

To decorate

grated chocolate

fresh mint sprigs

Method

❶ Pour the milk, coffee syrup, and peppermint syrup into a food processor and process gently until combined.

❷ Add the mint and ice cubes and process until a slushy consistency has been reached.

❸ Pour the mixture into 2 glasses. Sprinkle over the grated chocolate and decorate with fresh mint sprigs. Serve.

Drinks List